The E◆Z Legal Guide to

BANKRUPTCY

E◆Z LEGAL GUIDE

E◆Z Legal Books
Deerfield Beach, Florida

Printed in the United States of America

E·Z LEGAL FORMS®

384 South Military Trail Deerfield Beach, FL 33442
Tel. 954-480-8933 Fax 954-480-8906

Distributed by E-Z Legal Forms, Inc.

2 3 4 5 6 7 8 9 10

Library of Congress Catalog Card Number: 94-61621

The E-Z Legal Guide to Bankruptcy
p. cm.

ISBN 1-56382-400-0: $14.95

Title: The E-Z Legal Guide to Bankruptcy.

Bankruptcy

Important Facts

E-Z Legal products are designed to provide authoritative and accurate information in regard to the subject matter covered. However, neither this nor any other publication can take the place of an attorney on important legal matters.

Information in this guide has been carefully compiled from sources believed to be reliable, but the accuracy of the information is not guaranteed, as laws and regulations may change or be subject to differing interpretations.

Why not have your attorney review this guide? We encourage it.

Limited Warranty and Disclaimer

This is a self-help legal product and is intended to be used by the consumer for his or her own benefit. Use of this product to benefit a second party may be considered the unauthorized practice of law.

As with any legal matter, common sense should determine whether you need the assistance of an attorney. We urge you to consult with an attorney whenever large amounts of money are involved or on any matter when you do not understand how to properly complete a form or question its adequacy to protect you.

It is understood that by using this legal guide you are acting as your own attorney. Accordingly, the publisher, author, distributor and retailer shall have neither liability nor responsibility to any party for any loss or damage caused or alleged to be caused by use of this guide. This guide is sold with the understanding that the publisher, author, distributor and retailer are not engaged in rendering legal services. If legal services or other expert assistance are required, the services of a competent professional should be sought.

Money-back guarantee

E-Z Legal Forms offers you a limited guarantee. If E-Z Legal Forms are found to be defective, you may return your purchase and valid sales receipt to us within 30 days for a full refund of the list or purchase price, whichever is lower. In no event shall our liability – or the liability of any retailer – exceed the purchase price of the product. Use of the product constitutes acceptance of these terms.

Copyright Permission Certificate

The purchaser of this guide is hereby authorized to reproduce in any form or by any means, electronic or mechanical, including photocopying, all forms and documents contained in this guide, provided it is for nonprofit, educational or private use. Such reproduction requires no further permission from the publisher and/or payment of any permission fee.

The reproduction of any form or document in any other publication intended for sale is prohibited without the written permission of the publisher.

Publication for nonprofit use should provide proper attribution to E-Z Legal Forms.

Barry S. Chesler

Barry S. Chesler, President, E-Z Legal Forms

Bankruptcy

Table of contents

How to use this E-Z Legal Guide

E-Z Legal Guides can help you achieve an important legal objective conveniently, efficiently and economically. But it is nevertheless important for you to properly use this guide if you are to avoid later difficulties.

Step-by-step instructions for using this guide:

1. Carefully read all information, warnings and disclaimers concerning the legal forms in this guide. If after thorough examination you decide that you have circumstances that are not covered by the forms in this guide, or you do not feel confident about preparing your own documents, consult an attorney.
2. Before filling out a form, make several copies of the original to practice on, and for future use and updates. **All documents submitted to the court must be printed on one side only.** You should also make copies of the completed forms. Create a record-keeping system for both sets of copies.
3. Complete each blank on each legal form. Do not skip over inapplicable blanks or lines intended to be completed. If the blank is inapplicable, mark "N/A" or "None" or use a dash. This shows you have not overlooked the item.
4. Always use pen or type on legal documents. Never use pencil.
5. Avoid erasing or crossing out anything you've written on final documents.
6. It is important to remember that on legal contracts or agreements between parties all terms and conditions must be clearly stated. Provisions may not be enforceable unless in writing. All parties to the agreement should receive a copy.
7. You may find more specific instructions within this guide for completing some forms. These instructions are for your benefit and protection, so follow them closely.
8. You will find a helpful glossary of terms at the end of this guide. Refer to this glossary if you encounter unfamiliar terms.
9. Always keep legal documents in a safe place and in a location known to your spouse, family, personal representative or attorney.

CHAPTER 1

What is bankruptcy?

Simply stated, bankruptcy is a legal proceeding that allows you to get out of excessive debt and gain a fresh start financially. Bankruptcy is governed by federal law. The individual states have no important role in bankruptcy except that state laws, along with federal bankruptcy laws, determine the assets you may keep under a bankruptcy.

What are the different types of bankruptcy?

There are three common types of bankruptcy. To avoid confusion it is important to explain the purpose of each:

- **Chapter 7** allows either an individual or business to discharge virtually all unsecured debts. The debtor loses all property except that exempted by law. Most individuals in financial difficulty file under Chapter 7 of the Bankruptcy Code.
- **Chapter 13** is an alternative to Chapter 7 bankruptcy. It is designed for "wage earners" with relatively small amounts of consumer debt (as opposed to business debt). A debtor may file a Chapter 13 if he/she has $250,000 or less in unsecured debt and/or $750,000 or less in secured debt. Under a Chapter 13 bankruptcy, a debtor arranges to pay back all or part of his/her debts over a 3-to-5 year period. The advantage of a Chapter 13 is that the debtor loses no property.
- **Chapter 11** is for individuals or corporations engaged in business who desire to reorganize their debts, and seek court protection while they negotiate a plan of reorganization with creditors.

The forms in this guide can be used for a Chapter 7, Chapter 13 or Chapter 11 bankruptcy. This guide can be used for either personal or business bankruptcy.

Since there are numerous advantages and disadvantages to each type of bankruptcy, it is recommended that you discuss your options with an experienced bankruptcy attorney before you file a bankruptcy on your own.

A bankruptcy involving an operating business nearly always requires the services of an attorney. Moreover, a corporation cannot be represented by anyone other than an attorney, as it is considered a separate and distinct entity from its owners and officers. Therefore, unless you are an attorney, it is improper for you to file a bankruptcy for an incorporated business even though you may be its owner.

Since 90 percent of all bankruptcy filings are individuals filing a Chapter 7, or "straight" bankruptcy as it is sometimes called, the information in this booklet focuses primarily on this type of proceeding.

Highlight

Bankruptcy proceedings are usually initiated by the debtor filing a voluntary petition with the federal bankruptcy court. Anyone can file for bankruptcy notwithstanding their financial condition.

Who may file for bankruptcy?

Bankruptcy proceedings are usually initiated by the debtor filing a voluntary petition with the federal bankruptcy court. Anyone can file for bankruptcy notwithstanding their financial condition. This includes both natural persons and corporations. Only municipal corporations, railroads, insurance companies and certain savings institutions may not file for Chapter 7 bankruptcy. There are special bankruptcy provisions (Chapter 12 bankruptcy) for farmers.

Individuals and businesses operating as partnerships or corporations may be subject to an involuntary bankruptcy initiated by creditors. Certain individuals and businesses may not be forced into involuntary bankruptcy. These include ranchers and farmers, not-for-profit corporations, insurance companies, railroads, credit unions and savings and loan associations.

A debtor may be forced into involuntary bankruptcy only if the necessary number of creditors files an involuntary bankruptcy petition. If a debtor has 11 or fewer creditors, then any creditor owed at least $5,000 of unsecured debt may file an involuntary petition. An unsecured debt is one for which there is no collateral. If a debtor has more than 11 creditors, at least three creditors who are collectively owed $5,000 of unsecured debts must join together in filing an involuntary bankruptcy petition.

Additionally, before the court will accept the involuntary petition and issue an order of relief, the creditors must prove to the court that a debtor is either:

- not paying debts as they become due, or
- has entered into a non-bankruptcy liquidation proceeding within 120 days prior to the filing.

Creditors can also petition a debtor into bankruptcy under Chapter 11, although this is rare except in the case of larger corporate debtors. The vast majority of personal bankruptcies are voluntarily initiated by the debtor rather than filed by creditors as an involuntary petition.

Highlight

The vast majority of personal bankruptcies are voluntarily initiated by the debtor rather than filed by creditors as an involuntary petition.

If you are married and only one spouse has credit problems, you can choose to file bankruptcy individually. However, in most instances it's more advantageous to file jointly, because your spouse can be liable for your debts even if you file alone. When filing, you must indicate:

- whether you live in a community or common-law property state
- who owns the property
- which spouse is indebted to the creditor

The only community property states are Arizona, California, Idaho, Louisiana, Nevada, New Mexico, Texas, Washington, and Wisconsin. In common-law property states, the non-filing spouse may be liable for the debts incurred by the filing spouse if such debts were for basic living expenses such as food, shelter, clothing and utilities. In community property states, your spouse's share of the property may be taken by the creditor to pay your debts.

In addition, filing jointly allows married couples to double their federal exemptions. You must decide which exemptions to use – state or federal. If you use state exemptions, check with the federal bankruptcy court clerk in your area to determine whether you may double your state exemptions. Both spouses must use the same exemptions.

Note: If you are filing jointly in a Chapter 7, use only one *Chapter 7 Individual Debtor's Statement of Intention Form* for both spouses.

CHAPTER 2

Protection, exemption, and non-dischargeable debts

Whether you file under Chapter 7, 11 or 13, once a bankruptcy petition is filed it operates as an automatic stay. Generally, all debt collection or repossession activities by creditors must come to a halt. Likewise, all lawsuits must stop while the bankruptcy action is before the bankruptcy court. The purpose of the automatic stay is to transfer all collection and debtor-creditor matters to the bankruptcy court. For example, creditors may not enforce prior judgments or liens against either the debtor or his property. Criminal actions against the debtor do continue, as do actions for the collection of back alimony or child support.

Although the automatic stay suspends a creditor's right to repossess collateral, secured creditors can petition the bankruptcy court for a relaxation of this rule. This procedure is known as requesting adequate protection. A secured creditor is a creditor who holds specific property as collateral for repayment of a debt.

Should a secured creditor request adequate protection, the bankruptcy court will try to provide a remedy so the collateral is not impaired by the automatic stay. This would be important when the collateral is losing value over time. For example, if a debtor bought a boat that is being used by the debtor, the boat will likely decrease in value over time. Here, the court might require the debtor to make periodic cash payments to the secured party. In some cases the court will allow the creditor to repossess and sell the collateral if no other alternative seems to protect the creditor's interest. The automatic stay ends when the case is closed, dismissed or the debtor receives a discharge.

If you haven't already stopped making payments to creditors, you should stop once your bankruptcy petition is filed. You should, however, stay current on debts incurred after you filed the petition.

What property is exempt under a bankruptcy?

Under Chapter 7 bankruptcy, the trustee liquidates the debtor's assets for the benefit of the debtor's creditors. However, an individual is allowed to keep a certain amount of property. This "exempt" property allows the debtor to gain a fresh start.

The classification of property as either exempt or non-exempt is important to both the debtor and the creditors. Before 1978 the area of exemptions was strictly a matter of state law, and each state had its own list of exempt properties. In 1978 Congress decided the states could use a federal list of exemptions.

Highlight

In states that allow the debtor to file a list of exempt property according to either a state or federal list, you must take great care to determine which list will provide the greatest advantage.

Today some states require the debtor to use the state list of exemptions. Others offer an option: Residents filing bankruptcies may choose the federal list of exemptions or the state's list, depending on which is more advantageous to the resident.

For example, Social Security benefits are normally found on both state and federal bankruptcy exemption lists. But the value of a home that can be held out of the reach of creditors may differ between a state's list of exemptions and the federal list.

If your state offers the option, take care to determine which list will provide the greatest advantage to you. State exemptions may or may not be more generous than federal.

Appendixes 1 and 2 in the back of this manual list state and federal exemptions. Find your state, and note in the third category from the bottom of the page whether you have the option of claiming the federal exemptions. If you do, compare the federal list with your state's list in light of your circumstances.

The following is a summary of Appendix 1, the federal exemptions allowed.

- A homestead exemption not to exceed $15,000.
- A motor vehicle valued at $2,400 or less.
- $400 in value for specific items of household goods, furnishing and clothing or crops used by the debtor or his family for personal use up to an aggregate total of $8,000.
- Jewelry with a maximum value of $1,000.

- Real or personal property totaling no more than $800 individually and totaling up to $7,500 of unused homestead or burial plot exemptions.
- Tools or professional books valued up to $1,500.
- Life insurance contracts.
- Up to $8,000 in dividends, interest or loan value on a life insurance policy.
- Health aids, such as wheelchairs, etc.
- Future benefits, including Social Security, unemployment benefits, veterans benefits, alimony and child support.
- The right to compensation for lawsuits, including wrongful death benefits, insurance proceeds and compensation for bodily injury up to $15,000.

Highlight

If you have significant assets you should plan ahead for bankruptcy with your attorney or financial advisor.

Before filing for bankruptcy you may be wise to convert non-exempt property into exempt property. You may also decide to sell non-exempt property and use the proceeds to pay debts that would not be dischargeable in bankruptcy – such as alimony or non-dischargeable taxes.

These financial planning considerations are important. Therefore, if you have significant assets you should plan ahead for bankruptcy with your attorney or financial advisor.

The objective is to go into bankruptcy with as few non-exempt assets as possible. But remember, you must be totally honest in your disposal of assets, as the courts will closely scrutinize transfers made shortly before bankruptcy.

These exemptions do not apply under Chapter 11 or 13, as the objective in each instance is to keep all property and simply adjust the debt.

What debts are non-dischargeable in bankruptcy?

Debts in bankruptcy are considered either dischargeable or non-dischargeable.

Most debts are dischargeable under Chapter 7 bankruptcy. This means that you no longer have to pay the debt, which is deemed canceled.

Certain debts are not dischargeable by an individual in a Chapter 7 bankruptcy. Still other debts that are normally dischargeable may be denied a discharge because of wrongful actions of the debtor.

Debts that are non-dischargeable generally fall into the following categories:

- Individual income taxes that are assessed within three years of the filing but remain unpaid. Older taxes are dischargeable.
- Debts that have been incurred by the use of false financial statements or other false pretenses.
- Unscheduled debts (debts that the debtor failed to schedule on the bankruptcy petition).
- Debts that arise from fraud or embezzlement or from the misuse of funds when the debtor was acting as a fiduciary. Embezzling money from a trust fund over which the debtor has control is an example.
- Alimony maintenance and child support.
- Any debt incurred from willful or malicious conduct.
- Fines and penalties.
- Most educational loans (although a hardship exception allows a debtor to avoid certain educational loans).
- Debts over $500 for luxury goods or services when incurred within 40 days of the bankruptcy.
- Debts for cash advances in excess of $1,000 on credit cards, incurred within 20 days of the bankruptcy.
- Debts arising from a judgment incurred from a drunken driving conviction.
- Withholding taxes due by you as an officer of a company.

Highlight

Most debts are dischargeable under Chapter 7 bankruptcy. This means that you no longer have to pay the debt, which is deemed cancelled.

Debts are not discharged under either Chapter 11 or 13. In each instance the debts are only adjusted pursuant to a plan of repayment approved by a majority of creditors and the court. The plan may call for a reduction in the various classes of debt and/or an extension of time to pay the debts under the approved schedule. Any debts in excess of those approved by the plan are discharged.

Other debts that are normally dischargeable may be denied a discharge because of the actions of the debtor. One of the creditors may petition the court to deny the discharge on one specific debt, or on the entire bankruptcy, leaving the debtor without relief from creditor claims.

An individual debtor may be denied a discharge of debts for the following reasons:

- Hiding or destroying assets to hinder, delay or defraud a creditor.

- Failing to keep financial records or hiding or destroying financial records.
- Refusing to comply with an order of the bankruptcy court.
- Failing to provide a credible explanation for missing assets.
- Having had debts discharged in a Chapter 7 proceeding within the preceding 6 years.

It is important that you be totally honest in preparing your schedules and in handling your affairs both before and during the bankruptcy proceeding. Only then can you be assured that your debts will be discharged through bankruptcy.

Highlight

It is important that you be totally honest in preparing your schedules and in handling your affairs both before and during the bankruptcy proceeding.

CHAPTER

The filing procedure

3

When to file for bankruptcy

Timing is important when filing bankruptcy. You should be mindful of certain assets you will needlessly lose should you file at the wrong time. The trustee in bankruptcy, for example, has the right to claim:

- tax refunds due but not yet received
- insurance proceeds from pre-petition claims
- inheritances received within six months from the date of filing
- lawsuit proceeds arising from claims that pre-date the bankruptcy

In essence, you should ask yourself two questions before you file bankruptcy:

1) Have you collected all possible assets?
2) Have you converted as much of your net worth into exempt property as possible?

Only when these two objectives are accomplished are you ready to file for bankruptcy under Chapter 7.

How to file for bankruptcy

What to file

You must file with the Clerk of the Bankruptcy Court an original and five copies of the completed and signed forms for Chapter 7 and Chapter 13. You must file an original and six copies for Chapter 11. You must use official forms as are contained in this guide. Be certain that the original forms are neatly typed. You may photocopy additional sets of forms for filing. Bankruptcy courts may require the forms to be pre-punched with two holes at the top to facilitate the securing of the papers in the case file.

Where to file

You must file your bankruptcy in the bankruptcy court within the district where you resided during the preceding 180 days (or for the majority of the preceding 180 days).

Filing fee

The current filing fee for a Chapter 7 or Chapter 13 bankruptcy can range from $150 to $160. This must be paid upon filing by cash, certified check or bank check. If you are unable to pay the full amount upon filing, you may file an Application to Pay Filing Fee in Installments. The court will later instruct you as to your payment schedule. The filing fee for a Chapter 11 can range from $600 to $800. Ask the Bankruptcy Court Clerk for the correct fees in your district.

Highlight

You may, however, notify creditors of your filing earlier, particularly if it is necessary to stop creditor harassment.

Notice to your creditors

The court will notify your creditors of your bankruptcy filing within approximately two weeks of your filing. You may, however, notify creditors of your filing earlier, particularly if it is necessary to stop creditor harassment. Remember – once creditors learn of your bankruptcy they can take no further action to collect their debt.

First meeting of creditors

About three weeks following the filing of your petition, you will receive from the bankruptcy court a notice of the first meeting of creditors.

You must appear at this hearing. Otherwise your bankruptcy may be dismissed. If you cannot attend on the date and time specified, notify the bankruptcy court (and your bankruptcy trustee, identified in your notice) and request a continuance. Your request for continuance must be in writing, and should clearly state the name and number of your case.

At this hearing you will be asked general questions concerning your assets and other information contained on your bankruptcy schedule. Review your schedules in advance so you are prepared.

Answer all questions candidly and truthfully. Your trustee will conduct the hearing, although if any creditors are present they may also question you. Most first meetings for simple, personal bankruptcies are straightforward and last only a few minutes.

Amendments

You may, and indeed should, amend your bankruptcy petition should there be new information. For example, you should amend your petition to:

- reflect a change of address
- add assets you may have overlooked
- include creditors that you neglected to list when you first prepared the schedules
- correct any inaccuracies or misstatements in your original petition or schedules

Highlight

Most first meetings for simple, personal bankruptcies are straightforward and last only a few minutes.

If you file an amendment you must mail a copy of that amendment to your creditors, and this must be indicated on your amendment.

Objections to discharge

Should any creditor object to discharge, the creditor must file a formal complaint with the bankruptcy court. The creditor may seek to dismiss your entire bankruptcy or simply prevent the discharge of his specific debt. As stated earlier, a creditor can only object for good cause. Should such an objection be filed, it will be necessary to engage an attorney to defend against it.

Discharge hearing

Eventually you will receive notice of your discharge hearing. As with other hearings, you must be present. Usually your hearing will be held along with other debtors also undergoing discharge. At the hearing you will be advised of the effects of your bankruptcy.

Reaffirmation of debts

You may wish to reaffirm certain debts. Although you should be extremely cautious when deciding to reaffirm a debt, it is possible. It will be necessary to sign a reaffirmation, which must also be signed by your creditor. It will also be necessary to file the agreement in court and obtain approval of the bankruptcy judge, who will determine whether reaffirmation is in your best interests.

Debtors in Chapter 11 or 13 bankruptcy will undergo a more complex proceeding, as it will be necessary for the debtor to formulate a plan of reorganization (Chapter 11) or a wage earner plan (Chapter 13) that will, in each instance, require notice to the creditors of the proposed plan and court hearings to confirm the plan. Due to their complexity, it is strongly suggested that Chapter 11 and Chapter 13 debtors retain legal counsel.

Bankruptcy

Glossary of useful terms

A-C

Adequate Protection – The standard of protection granted a creditor by the trustee or debtor-in-possession to prevent the court from allowing the creditor to foreclose on its property.

Automatic Stay – An injunction, or court order, that takes effect when a bankruptcy petition is filed. An automatic stay prohibits all collection action against a debtor.

Avoidance Powers – The powers used by a trustee to reverse transfers of the debtor's property.

Balance Sheet – A statement of financial conditions as of a specific date. It is different from a cash flow statement, which summarizes income and expenses.

Bankruptcy Code – The body of a federal statutory law that governs the bankruptcy process.

Bankruptcy Petition – The legal instrument filed with the bankruptcy court that commences a bankruptcy proceeding.

Bar Date – The last date for filing a proof of claim.

Chapter 7 – In a Chapter 7 proceeding, the debtor's business is liquidated and its assets are distributed to creditors with allowed proofs of claims.

Chapter 11 – Normally, a Chapter 11 proceeding is a reorganization proceeding. The debtor continues to operate its business after the bankruptcy is filed. Chapter 11 liquidations are commonplace, and usually result from an unsuccessful reorganization attempt.

C-D

Chapter 11 Plan – In a Chapter 11 proceeding, the reorganization plan sets forth the rights of all classes of creditors. It may also include various repayment schedules pertaining to the various creditors.

Chapter 13 – May only be filed by an individual debtor with limited debt. In essence, it allows a payment plan for an individual's financial and/or business debts.

Closing – When a bankruptcy case is closed, it is no longer on the court's docket.

Collateral – Property of a debtor in which a creditor has a lien securing its debt.

Complaint – A pleading that is filed to initiate a lawsuit or an adversary proceeding.

Composition – Out-of-court agreement to pay a percentage of a debt in full settlement.

Consumer Credit Counseling Services – Non-profit organizations established to help debtors make payment arrangements with creditors.

Contingent Claim – A claim, debt or obligation arising from involvement in a transaction that may or may not become due at a future date; for example, co-signing a loan and the principal defaults.

Conversion – The conversion of a bankruptcy case from one chapter type to another.

Cram-Down – The confirmation of a plan to reorganize over the objection of a creditor or class of creditors by the votes of other creditors.

Creditor – One to whom you owe money.

Debtor – One who owes debts. In bankruptcy, the bankrupt business that is under the control and protection of the bankruptcy court is the debtor.

Debtor-in-Possession (DIP) – The business debtor in a Chapter 11 reorganization. In a Chapter 11, either the debtor or a trustee is in control of the business or assets.

Discharge – A discharge in bankruptcy relieves the debtor of the dischargeable debts incurred prior to filing. Discharge is the legal term for the elimination of debt through bankruptcy.

D-L

Dismissal – The dismissal of a bankruptcy case, for all intents and purposes, returns the debtor to the same place it was before bankruptcy was filed.

Disputed Claim – A debt that is or may be asserted against you but for which you contest liability.

Examiner – An officer of the court sometimes appointed to investigate the financial affairs of the debtor.

Exemption or Exempt Property – Property of an individual debtor that the law protects from the actions of creditors, such as the debtor's residence or homestead, automobile and the like.

Fiduciary -- A person placed in a position of special trust, such as when transacting business or handling property for another person.

Foreclosure – A debt-collection procedure whereby property of the debtor is sold on the courthouse steps to satisfy debts. Foreclosure often involves real estate of the debtor.

General, Unsecured Claim – A claim that is neither secured nor granted a priority by the Bankruptcy Code. Most trade debts are general, unsecured claims.

Involuntary Bankruptcy Proceeding – In an involuntary bankruptcy proceeding the debtor is forced into bankruptcy by creditors. Involuntary bankruptcies are relatively rare.

Judicial Lien – A lien created by the order of a court, such as the lien created by taking a judgment against a debtor.

Jurisdiction – The power and authority of a court to issue binding orders after hearing controversies.

Levy and Execution – A judicial debt-collection procedure in which the court orders the sheriff to seize the debtor's property found in the county to sell in satisfaction of the debtor's debt or debts.

Lien – An interest in property securing the repayment of a debt.

Liquidated Debt – A debt is liquidated when it is certain what is due and how much is due.

M-S

Motion – A request for the court to act. A motion may be filed within a lawsuit, adversary proceeding or bankruptcy case.

Personal Property – Moveable property. Property that is not permanently attached to land is considered personalty.

Petition for Relief – The papers filed initiating a bankruptcy case.

Possessory Security Interest – A security interest or lien on property that requires the creditor to have possession of the property, such as a pawn or pledge.

Preference – A transfer of property of the debtor to a creditor made immediately prior to the debtor's bankruptcy, which enables the creditor to receive more than it would have received from the bankruptcy. A preferential transfer must be made while the debtor was insolvent and as payment for a debt that existed prior to the transfer of property.

Priority – Certain categories of claims are designated as priority claims by the Bankruptcy Code, such as claims for lost wages or taxes. Each classification of claims must be paid in order of priority (the claims in one class must be paid in full before the next class receives any payment).

Priority Proof of Claim or Priority Claim – A proof of claim of the type granted priority by the Bankruptcy Code.

Proof of Claim – The document filed in a bankruptcy case that establishes a creditor's claim for payment against the debtor.

Reaffirmation – An agreement between creditor and debtor in which the debtor voluntarily agrees to repay the debt.

Realty or Real Property – Immoveable property, such as land and/or buildings attached to land.

Redemption – The right of a debtor in a bankruptcy to purchase certain real or personal property from a secured creditor by paying the current value of the property (regardless of the amount owed on the property).

Secured Creditor – A creditor whose debt is secured by a lien on property of the debtor.

S-U

Secured Proof of Claim – A proof of claim for a debt that is secured by a lien, a judgment or other security interest.

Security Interest – A lien on the property in the possession of the debtor that acts as security for the debt owed to the creditor.

Statutory Lien – A lien created by operation of law, such as a mechanic's lien or a tax lien. A statutory lien does not require the consent of the parties or a court order.

Trustee – An officer of the court appointed to take custody of the assets of a bankruptcy estate.

Unliquidated Debt – A claim, debt or obligation remaining unassessed or unsettled because of uncertainty about how much is due.

Unsecured Creditor – A creditor without security for its debt.

The forms in this guide

This kit contains all the forms customarily required to process a Chapter 7, 11 or 13 bankruptcy.

It is important to note that you may not require use of all forms, as some are for the different types of bankruptcy or are for use by creditors. For this reason it is important to carefully read the instructions for each form. The forms are listed in the order in which they should be presented to the court.

You will find the following forms in this guide:

- ***Notice to Individual Consumer Debtor(s)*** – This is generally completed by the Clerk of the Bankruptcy Court and confirms that you have been advised of the various types of bankruptcy that are available to you.
- ***Statement of Attorney for Petitioner*** – If you have an attorney, this form will be completed by your attorney and is intended to advise the court of the compensation paid to counsel and agreed to be paid later. All legal fees in a bankruptcy must be court approved.
- ***Disclosure of Compensation of Bankruptcy Petition Preparer*** – This is similar in purpose to the prior form pertaining to attorneys, but applies to any non-attorney assistance you may have had in preparing your bankruptcy.
- ***Voluntary Petition*** – This simple form applies to all bankruptcies. First, fill in the top portion of the form. Type your address, including your county, on the line in the appropriate box of the form. An example would be: "10 Elm Street, Boston, MA 11111 Suffolk County."

Next, insert the date on the line where indicated. Sign your name on the line at the bottom of the form. If you are married and are filing the petition together, your spouse should also complete the joint debtor section of the petition and sign it. All sections of the petition must be completed. If you have no information for a particular box, you should indicate by stating "none."

- ***Filing of Plan*** – This form must be completed in all types of bankruptcy cases, but the section of the form marked "Filing of Plan" does not apply to Chapter 7 cases.
- ***Exhibit "A" to Voluntary Petition*** – Exhibit A is to be completed when the debtor is a business and filing for Chapter 11.
- ***Application to Pay Filing Fees in Installments*** – The bankruptcy court may allow you time to pay your filing fee in installments. If you need time, complete and submit the form. This does not apply to Chapter 11 business reorganizations.
- ***List of Creditors Holding 20 Largest Unsecured Claims*** – This must be completed only in a Chapter 11 reorganization. It can be disregarded in all other proceedings.
- ***Summary of Schedules*** – This is to be completed in all bankruptcy proceedings. Since it summarizes your various schedules, you will want to complete each individual schedule first. Each schedule is self-explanatory, with adequate instructions for completion. They occur as:
  - Schedule A Real Property
  - Schedule B Personal Property
  - Schedule C Property Claimed as Exempt. This schedule requires simple legal research to cite the state or federal law that allows each exemption.
  - Schedule D Creditors Holding Secured Claims
  - Schedule E Creditors Holding Unsecured Priority Claims
  - Schedule F Creditors Holding Unsecured Non-Priority Claims
  - Schedule G Executory Contracts and Unexpired Leases
  - Schedule H Co-debtors
  - Schedule I Current Income of Individual Debtors
  - Schedule J Current Expenditures of Individual Debtors
- ***Declaration Concerning Debtor's Schedules*** – This form attests

to the truthfulness of all the schedules, and applies to all bankruptcies. Be certain your schedules include all known assets, as there can be serious consequences for concealment.

- ***Statement of Financial Affairs*** – This contains nine pages. If a question does not apply, mark the box "none." Be complete and accurate in all information provided. The Statement of Financial Affairs is required in all bankruptcies.
- ***Chapter 7 Individual Debtor's Statement of Intention*** – This applies only to Chapter 7 cases filed by individuals, whether engaged in business or not. In part b of this form, please note the following definitions:

  §522(f) - provides that a debtor may petition the court to remove a lien that has been placed upon exempt property. This changes a secured creditor into an unsecured one.

  §524(c) - states that even though a debt has been discharged, the debtor voluntarily chooses to repay that debt. This agreement must be in writing and filed with the court.

  §722 - deals with avoiding liens through redemption. The debtor is allowed to redeem or regain possession of any tangible personal property that is intended primarily for household, family or personal use if that property is claimed as exempt under §522 or has been abandoned by the trustee. The property may be redeemed by paying the lienholder the current value of the property, not the amount of the secured claim.

Highlight

Be certain your schedules include all known assets, as there can be serious consequences for concealment.

- ***Master Mailing List*** **(Matrix Form)** – This is used to list all creditors. It must be filed in all bankruptcy cases. Note instructions on reverse side. It is also wise to check requirements with the Clerk of the Bankruptcy Court, as various courts impose different requirements for the preparation of the creditor list.

This concludes the documents you must prepare and file with the bankruptcy court to initiate your bankruptcy. There are in this guide, however, several additional forms which may be useful:

- ***Notice of Commencement of Case*** – This form is ordinarily provided by the bankruptcy court and completed by the clerk. There is a separate notice for Chapter 7, 11 and 13 proceedings.
- ***Discharge of Debtor*** – This can be used only on a Chapter 7 bankruptcy. Most bankruptcy courts issue their own discharge documents, and therefore this form may not be required.

- ***Debtor's Plan and Motion to Avoid Liens*** – This form is used in Chapter 13. It describes the debtor's installments paid to creditors.

Errors to avoid

Because bankruptcy courts increasingly rely upon sophisticated computer equipment, it is necessary to avoid certain procedures, particularly in completing lists of creditors, where the court must use a scanner to read and reprint the names and addresses of creditors for notification purposes.

Bankruptcy courts may impose some additional local rules in regard to the filing requirements within their jurisdiction. For that reason it is recommended that you review the filing requirements with the Clerk of the Bankruptcy Court and that you file well in advance of any required stay against creditors.

Highlight

It is recommended that you review the filing requirements with the Clerk of the Bankruptcy Court and that you file well in advance of any required stay against creditors.

Please avoid the following mistakes on your paperwork:

1. **Extra marks on forms.** Do not use letterhead or file forms with dates, debtor's name, coffee stains, handwritten marks, extra lines, page numbers, etc.
2. **Non-standard paper,** such as onion skin, odd-sized or colored paper (such as buff or yellow).
3. **Poor quality type** caused by submitting a photocopy or carbon copy or using a worn-out typewriter or one with an old ribbon.
4. **Bold type.** Do not use a bold setting on your typewriter or printer.
5. **Unreadable type faces** or print styles, such as proportionally spaced fonts, dot-matrix printing or exotic fonts such as Olde English or Script. Use only Courier 10, Prestige Elite or Letter Gothic.
6. **Improperly aligned lists** caused by removing the paper from the typewriter before completing the list, or by inserting the paper into the typewriter crooked.
7. **Incorrect typewriter settings.** Make certain that your typewriter is set for 10 pitch if you are using a 10 pitch typestyle.
8. **All uppercase (capital letters) should be avoided.** Type in upper and lower case as you would a letter.
9. **Zip code must be on the last line.** Nine-digit zip codes should be typed with a hyphen separating the two groups of digits. Do not

type "to the attention of" lines or account numbers on the last line of an address. If needed, put these on the second line between the name and address. The zip code must be at the end for the zip code sorting equipment to find it.

10. **Typing numbers.** Do not substitute a lowercase "L" for the number "1."
11. **Two-sided forms.** The forms in this guide are printed on both sides. Copy each form you need as a single-sided document which many courts require.

Notice: After deciding which forms your bankruptcy case requires, copy the blank forms as one-sided documents. We suggest making several copies for worksheets as well. You should also make a copy of the finished forms to retain for your files.

United States Bankruptcy Court

NOTICE TO INDIVIDUAL CONSUMER DEBTOR(S)

The purpose of this notice is to acquaint you with the four chapters of the federal Bankruptcy Code under which you may file a bankruptcy petition. The bankruptcy law is complicated and not easily described. Therefore, you should seek the advice of an attorney to learn of your rights and responsibilities under the law should you decide to file a petition with the court. Court employees are prohibited from giving you legal advice.

Chapter 7: Liquidation ($130 filing fee plus $30 administrative fee)

1. Chapter 7 is designed for debtors in financial difficulty who do not have the ability to pay their existing debts.

2. Under Chapter 7 a trustee takes possession of all your property. You may claim certain of your property as exempt under governing law. The trustee then liquidates the property and uses the proceeds to pay your creditors according to priorities of the Bankruptcy Code.

3. The purpose of filing a Chapter 7 case is to obtain a discharge of your existing debts. If, however, you are found to have committed certain kinds of improper conduct described in the Bankruptcy Code, your discharge may be denied by the court, and the purpose for which you filed the bankruptcy petition will be defeated.

4. Even if you receive a discharge, there are some debts that are not discharged under the law. Therefore, you may still be responsible for such debts as certain taxes and student loans, alimony and support payments, criminal restitution, and debts for death or personal injury caused by driving while intoxicated from alcohol or drugs.

5. Under certain circumstances you may keep property that you have purchased subject to valid security interest. Your attorney can explain the options that are available to you.

Chapter 11: Reorganization ($800 filing fee)

Chapter 11 is designed primarily for the reorganization of a business but is also available to consumer debtors. Its provisions are quite complicated, and any decision by an individual to file a Chapter 11 petition should be reviewed with an attorney.

Chapter 12: Family Farmer ($200 filing fee)

Chapter 12 is designed to permit family farmers to repay their debts over a period of time from future earnings and is in many ways similar to Chapter 13. The eligibility requirements are restrictive, limiting its use to those whose income arises primarily from a family-owned farm.

Chapter 13: Repayment of All or Part of the Debts of an Individual with Regular Income ($130 filing fee plus $30 administrative fee)

1. Chapter 13 is designed for individuals with regular income who are temporarily unable to pay their debts but would like to pay them in installments over a period of time. You are only eligible for Chapter 13 if your debts do not exceed certain dollar amounts set forth in the Bankruptcy Code.

2. Under Chapter 13 you must file a plan with the court to repay your creditors all or part of the money that you owe them, using your future earnings. Usually, the period allowed by the court to repay your debts is three years, but no more than five years. Your plan must be approved by the court before it can take effect.

3. Under Chapter 13, unlike Chapter 7, you may keep all your property, both exempt and non-exempt, as long as you continue to make payments under the plan.

4. After completion of payments under your plan, your debts are discharged except alimony and support payments, student loans, certain debts including criminal fines and restitution and debts for death or personal injury caused by driving while intoxicated from alcohol or drugs, and long-term secured obligations.

I, the debtor, affirm that I have read this notice.

______________________	______________________	______________________
Date	Signature of Debtor	Case Number

Name ______________________________

Address ______________________________

____

Telephone ______________________________

☐ Attorney for Debtor(s) | (If applicable) Attorney's

☐ Debtor Representing Self | State Bar I.D. No. __________

UNITED STATES BANKRUPTCY COURT
__________________ DISTRICT OF __________________

In re ______________________________,

[Set forth here all names including married, maiden, and trade names used by debtor within last 6 years.]

Debtor

Case No.__________________

Chapter__________________

Social Security No(s).__________________and all
Employer's Tax Identification Nos.*[if any]* __________

____

STATEMENT OF ATTORNEY FOR PETITIONER PURSUANT TO BANKRUPTCY RULE 2016(b)

The undersigned, pursuant to Rule 2016(b), Bankruptcy Rules, states that:

(1) The undersigned, is the attorney for the debtor(s) in this case.

(2) The compensation paid or agreed to be paid by the debtor(s) in this case.

- (a) for legal services rendered or to be rendered in contemplation of and in connection with this case... $__________
- (b) prior to filing this statement, debtor(s) have paid.................. $__________
- (c) the unpaid balance due and payable is.................. $__________

(3) $__________________of the filing fee in this case has been paid.

(4) The services rendered or to be rendered include the following:

- (a) Analysis of the financial situation, and rendering advice and assistance to the debtor(s) in determining whether to file a petition under Title 11, United States Code.
- (b) Preparation and filing of the petition, schedules of assets and liabilities, statement of affairs, and other documents required by the court.
- (c) Representation of the debtor(s) at the first meeting of creditors, confirmation hearing, Relief from Stay, and compliance with General Order No. 1.
- (d) Attorney may seek supplemental fees for Relief from Stay hearings;

(5) The source of payments made by the debtor(s) to the undersigned was from earnings, wages and compensation for services performed, and if a fee is paid by transfer of property or if security is taken, give details here and in appropriate Section of Schedules or Statement of Affairs.

(6) The source of payments to be made by the debtor(s) to the undersigned for the unpaid balance remaining, if any, will be from earnings, wages and compensation for services performed, and

(7) The undersigned have not shared or agreed to share, with any other person, other than with members of their law firm or corporation, any compensation paid or to be paid except as follows:

Dated:______________________________ ______________________________

____

Attorneys for Debtor(s)

UNITED STATES BANKRUPTCY COURT

_____________ District of _______________

In re: ______________________________ Bankruptcy Case No.___________________
Debtor Chapter __________

Address:
Social Security No(s).:
Employer's Tax Identification No(s).[if any]:

DISCLOSURE OF COMPENSATION OF BANKRUPTCY PETITION PREPARER

1. Under 11 U.S.C. §110(h), I declare under penalty of perjury that I am not an attorney or employee of an attorney, that I prepared or caused to be prepared one or more documents for filing by the above-named debtor(s) in connection with this bankruptcy case, and that compensation paid to me within one year before the filing of the bankruptcy petition, or agreed to be paid to me, for services rendered on behalf of the debtor(s) in contemplation of or in connection with the bankruptcy case is as follows:

For document preparation services, I have agreed to accept................................ $_______________

Prior to the filing of this statement I have received .... $_______________

Balance due.. $_______________

2. I have prepared or caused to be prepared the following documents (itemize):

   and provided the following services (itemize):

3. The source of the compensation paid to me was:

   ☐ Debtor ☐ Other (specify)

4. The source of compensation to be paid to me is:

   ☐ Debtor ☐ Other (specify)

5. The foregoing is a complete statement of any agreement or arrangement for payment to me for preparation of the petition filed by the debtor(s) in this bankruptcy case.

6. To my knowledge no other person has prepared for compensation a document for filing in connection with this bankruptcy case except as listed below:

   NAME SOCIAL SECURITY NUMBER

DECLARATION OF BANKRUPTCY PETITION PREPARER

I declare under penalty of perjury that the foregoing is true and correct to the best of my knowledge, information, and belief.

x______________________________ ______________________________ ____________

Signature | Social Security Number | Date

Name (Print):______________________________

Address: ______________________________

____

____

A bankruptcy petition preparer's failure to comply with the provisions of Title 11 and the Federal Rules of Bankruptcy Procedure may result in fines or imprisonment or both. 11 U.S.C. §110; 18 U.S.C. §156.

United States Bankruptcy Court
District of

VOLUNTARY PETITION

IN RE (Name of debtor-If individual, enter Last, First, Middle)

NAME OF JOINT DEBTOR (Spouse) (Last, First, Middle)

ALL OTHER NAMES used by the debtor in the last 6 years (including married, maiden and trade names)

ALL OTHER NAMES used by the joint debtor in the last 6 years (include married, maiden and trade names)

SOC. SEC./TAX I.D. NO. (If more than one, state all)

SOC. SEC./TAX I.D. NO. (If more than one, state all)

STREET ADDRESS OF DEBTOR (No. and street, city, state, zip)

COUNTY OF RESIDENCE OR PRINCIPAL PLACE OF BUSINESS

STREET ADDRESS OF JOINT DEBTOR (No. and street, city, state, zip)

COUNTY OF RESIDENCE OR PRINCIPAL PLACE OF BUSINESS

MAILING ADDRESS OF DEBTOR (If different from street address)

MAILING ADDRESS OF JOINT DEBTOR (If different from street address)

LOCATION OF PRINCIPAL ASSETS OF BUSINESS DEBTOR
(If different from addresses listed above)

VENUE (Check one box)

☐ Debtor has been domiciled or has had a residence, principal place of business or principal assets in this Distrcit for 180 days immediately preceding the date of this petition or for a longer part of such 180 days than in any other District.

☐ There is a bankruptcy case concerning debtor's affiliate, general partner or partnership pending in this District

INFORMATION REGARDING DEBTOR (Check applicable boxes)

TYPE OF DEBTOR (Check one box)

☐ Individual
☐ Joint (H&W)
☐ Partnership
☐ Other ______________________
☐ Corporation Publicly Held
☐ Corporation Not Publicly Held
☐ Municipality

NATURE OF DEBT (Check one box)

☐ Non-Business Consumer
☐ Business - Complete A&B below

A. TYPE OF BUSINESS (Check one box)

☐ Farming
☐ Professional
☐ Retail/Wholesale
☐ Railroad
☐ Transportation
☐ Manufacturing/Mining
☐ Stockbroker
☐ Other Business
☐ Commodity Broker
☐ Construction
☐ Real Estate

B. BRIEFLY DESCRIBE NATURE OF BUSINESS

CHAPTER OR SECTION OF BANKRUPTCY CODE UNDER WHICH THE PETITION IS FILED (Check one box)

☐ Chapter 7
☐ Chapter 9
☐ Chapter 11
☐ Chapter 12
☐ Chapter 13
☐ §304-Case Ancillary to Foreign Proceeding

SMALL BUSINESS (Chapter 11 only)

☐ Debtor is a small business as defined in 11 U.S.C. §101.

☐ Debtor is and elects to be considered a small business under 11 U.S.C. §1121(e). (optional)

FILING FEE (Check one box)

☐ Filing fee attached

☐ Filing fee to be paid in installments. (Applicable to individuals only) Must attach signed application for the court's consideration certifying that the debtor is unable to pay fee except in installments. Rule 1006(b); see page K100-07.

NAME AND ADDRESS OF LAW FIRM OR ATTORNEY

Telephone No.

NAME(S) OF ATTORNEY(S) DESIGNATED TO REPRESENT THE DEBTOR (Print or Type)

STATISTICAL ADMINISTRATIVE INFORMATION (28 U.S.C. §604)
(Estimates only) (Check applicable boxes)

☐ Debtor estimates that funds will be available for distribution to unsecured creditors.

☐ Debtor estimates that after any exempt property is excluded and administrative expenses paid, there will be no funds available for distribution to unsecured creditors.

☐ Debtor is not represented by an attorney. Telephone no. of debtor not represented by an attorney: (   )

ESTIMATED NUMBER OF CREDITORS
☐ 1-15 ☐ 16-49 ☐ 50-99 ☐ 100-199 ☐ 200-999 ☐ 1000-over

ESTIMATED ASSETS (in thousands of dollars)
☐ Under 50 ☐ 50-99 ☐ 100-499 ☐ 500-999 ☐ 1000-9999 ☐ 10,000-99,000 ☐ 100,000-over

ESTIMATED LIABILITIES (in thousands of dollars)
☐ Under 50 ☐ 50-99 ☐ 100-499 ☐ 500-999 ☐ 1000-9999 ☐ 10,000-99,000 ☐ 100,000-over

ESTIMATED NUMBER OF EMPLOYEES - CH 11 & 12 ONLY
☐ 0 ☐ 1-19 ☐ 20-99 ☐ 100-999 ☐ 1000-over

ESTIMATED NO. OF EQUITY HOLDERS - CH 11 & 12 ONLY
☐ 0 ☐ 1-19 ☐ 20-99 ☐ 100-999 ☐ 1000-over

THIS SPACE FOR COURT USE ONLY

Name of Debtor ______________________________

Case No.______________________________

FILING OF PLAN

For Chapter 9, 11, 12 and 13 cases only. Check appropriate box.

I A copy of debtor's proposed plan dated ____________________ is attached.

☐ Debtor intends to file a plan within the time allowed by statute, rule, or order of the court.

PRIOR BANKRUPTCY CASE FILED WITHIN LAST 6 YEARS (If more than one, attach additional sheet)

Location Where Filed	Case Number	Date Filed

PENDING BANKRUPTCY CASE FILED BY ANY SPOUSE, PARTNER, OR AFFILIATE OF THIS DEBTOR (If more than one, attach additional sheet)

Name of Debtor	Case Number	Date
Relationship	**District**	**Judge**

REQUEST FOR RELIEF

Debtor requests relief in accordance with the chapter of Title 11, United States Code, specified in this petition.

SIGNATURES

ATTORNEY

X______________________________
Signature

____
Date

INDIVIDUAL/JOINT DEBTOR(S)

I declare under penalty of perjury that the information provided in this petition is true and correct.

X______________________________
Signature of Debtor

____
Date

X______________________________
Signature of Joint Debtor

____
Date

CORPORATE OR PARTNERSHIP DEBTOR

I declare under penalty of perjury that the information provided in this petition is true and correct, and that the filing of the petition on behalf of the debtor has been authorized.

X______________________________
Signature of Authorized Individual

____
Print or Type Name of Authorized Individual

____
Title of Individual Authorized by Debtor to File this Petition

____
Date

EXHIBIT "A" (To be completed if debtor is a corporation requesting relief under Chapter 11.)

☐ Exhibit "A" is attached and made a part of this petition.

TO BE COMPLETED BY INDIVIDUAL CHAPTER 7 DEBTOR WITH PRIMARILY CONSUMER DEBTS (SEE P.L. 98-353 § 322)

I am aware that I may proceed under chapter 7, 11, 12, or 13 of Title 11, United States Code. I understand the relief available under each such chapter, and choose to proceed under Chapter 7 of such title.

If I am represented by an attorney, exhibit "B" has been completed.

X______________________________
Signature of Debtor

____
Date

X______________________________
Signature of Joint Debtor

____
Date

EXHIBIT "B" (To be completed by attorney for individual Chapter 7 debtor(s) with primarily consumer debts.)

I, the attorney for the debtor(s) named in the foregoing petition, declare that I have informed the debtor(s) that (he, she, or they) may proceed under Chapter 7, 11, 12, or 13 of Title 11, United States Code, and have explained the relief available under each such chapter.

X______________________________
Signature of Attorney

____
Date

CERTIFICATION AND SIGNATURE OF NON-ATTORNEY BANKRUPTCY PETITION PREPARER (See 11 U.S.C. § 110)

I certify that I am a bankruptcy petition preparer as defined in 11 U.S.C. § 110, that I have prepared this document for compensation, and that I have provided the debtor with a copy of this document.

____
Printed or Typed Name of Bankruptcy Petition Preparer

____
Social Security Number

____

____
Address Tel. No.

Names and Social Security Numbers of all other individuals who prepared or assisted in preparing this document:

X______________________________
Signature of Bankruptcy Petition Preparer

If more than one person prepared this document, attach additional signed sheets conforming to the appropriate Official Form for each person.

A bankruptcy petition preparer's failure to comply with the provisions of Title 11 and the Federal Rules of Bankruptcy Procedure may result in fines or imprisonment or both. 11 U.S.C. § 110; 18 U.S.C. § 156.

UNITED STATES BANKRUPTCY COURT
______________ DISTRICT OF ______________

In re ____
Debtor   Case No. ____________________

Chapter _____________________

Exhibit "A" to Voluntary Petition

1. Debtor's employer identification number is _________________.

2. If any of debtor's securities are registered under section 12 of the Securities and Exchange Act of 1934, the SEC file number is _________________________.

3. The following financial data is the latest available information and refers to debtor's condition on _________________.

a. Total assets	$____________________________	
b. Total liabilities	$____________________________	
		Approximate number of holders
Fixed, liquidated secured debt	$________	___________
Contingent secured debt	$________	___________
Disputed secured claims	$________	___________
Unliquidated secured debt	$________	___________
		Approximate number of holders
Fixed, liquidated unsecured debt	$________	___________
Contingent unsecured debt	$________	___________
Disputed unsecured claims	$________	___________
Unliquidated unsecured debt	$________	___________
Number of shares of preferred stock	________	___________
Number of shares of common stock	________	___________

Comments, if any:____
____
____
____

4. Brief description of debtor's business:____
____
____

(Continued on next sheet)

5. List the name of any person who directly or indirectly owns, controls, or holds, with power to vote, 20% or more of the voting securities of debtor:____________________________________

____

____

____

6. List the names of all corporations of which 20% or more of the outstanding voting securities are directly or indirectly owned, controlled, or held, with power to vote, by debtor:__________________

____

____

____

DECLARATION UNDER PENALTY OF PERJURY ON BEHALF OF A CORPORATION OR PARTNERSHIP

I [the president *or* other officer *or* an authorized agent of the corporation] [*or* a member *or* an authorized agent of the partnership] named as the debtor in this case, declare under penalty of perjury that I have read the foregoing Exhibit "A" and that it is true and correct to the best of my information and belief.

Date ______________________________

Signature ______________________________

____

(Print Name and Title)

UNITED STATES BANKRUPTCY COURT

_______________ DISTRICT OF _______________

In re____,
Debtor

Case No.________________

Chapter________________

APPLICATION TO PAY FILING FEES IN INSTALLMENTS

In accordance with Fed. R. Bankr. P. 1006, application is made for permission to pay the filing fee on the following terms:

$ ____________________ with the filing of the petition, and the balance of

$ ____________________ in ____ installments, as follows:

$ ____________________ on or before ________________________

$ ____________________ on or before ________________________

$ ____________________ on or before ________________________

$ ____________________ on or before ________________________

I certify that I am unable to pay the filing fee except in installments. I further certify that I have not paid any money or transferred any property to an attorney or any other person for services in connection with this case or in connection with any other pending bankruptcy case and that I will not make any payment or transfer any property for services in connection with the case until the filing fee is paid in full.

Date: ________________________ ________________________________
Applicant

____
Address of Applicant

____

ORDER

IT IS ORDERED that the debtor pay the filing fee in installments on the terms set forth in the foregoing application.

IT IS FURTHER ORDERED that until the filing fee is paid in full the debtor shall not pay, and no person shall accept, any money for services in connection with this case, and the debtor shall not relinquish, and no person shall accept, any property as payment for services in connection with this case.

BY THE COURT

Date: ________________________ ________________________________
United States Bankruptcy Judge

UNITED STATES BANKRUPTCY COURT
_______________ DISTRICT OF _______________

In re____,
Debtor

Case No.____________________

Chapter____________________

LIST OF CREDITORS HOLDING 20 LARGEST UNSECURED CLAIMS

Following is the list of the debtor's creditors holding the 20 largest unsecured claims. The list is prepared in accordance with Fed. R. Bankr. P. 1007(d) for filing in this chapter 11 [*or* chapter 9] case. The list does not include (1) persons who come within the definition of "insider" set forth in 11 U.S.C. § 101(30), or (2) secured creditors unless the value of the collateral is such that the unsecured deficiency places the creditor among the holders of the 20 largest unsecured claims.

(1)	(2)	(3)	(4)	(5)
Name of creditor and complete mailing address including zip code	*Name, telephone number and complete mailing address, including zip code, of employee, agent, or department of creditor familiar with claim who may be contacted*	*Nature of claim (trade debt, bank loan, government contract, etc.)*	*Indicate if claim is contingent, unliquidated, disputed or subject to setoff*	*Amount of claim [if secured also state value of security]*

(Continued on next sheet)

In re ________________________________ Case No. ____________________

LIST OF CREDITORS HOLDING 20 LARGEST UNSECURED CLAIMS

(Continued)

(1)	(2)	(3)	(4)	(5)
Name of creditor and complete mailing address including zip code	*Name, telephone number and complete mailing address, including zip code, of employee, agent, or department of creditor familiar with claim who may be contacted*	*Nature of claim (trade debt, bank loan, government contract, etc.)*	*Indicate if claim is contingent, unliquidated, disputed or subject to setoff*	*Amount of claim [if secured also state value of security]*

DECLARATION UNDER PENALTY OF PERJURY ON BEHALF OF A CORPORATION OR PARTNERSHIP

I, [the president *or* other officer *or* an authorized agent of the corporation] [*or* a member *or* an authorized agent of the partnership] named as the debtor in this case, declare under penalty of perjury that I have read the foregoing "List of Creditors Holding 20 Largest Unsecured Claims" and that it is true and correct to the best of my information and belief.

Date____________________________

Signature____________________________

____

(Print Name and Title)

United States Bankruptcy Court

_______________ DISTRICT OF _______________

In re_______________________________, Case No.______________________
Debtor (If known)

SUMMARY OF SCHEDULES

Indicate as to each schedule whether that schedule is attached and state the number of pages in each. Report the totals from Schedules A,B,D,E,F,I, and J in the boxes provided. Add the amounts from Schedules A and B to determine the total amount of the debtor's assets. Add the amounts from Schedules D,E, and F to determine the total amount of the debtor's liabilities.

NAME OF SCHEDULE	ATTACHED (YES/NO)	NO. OF SHEETS	AMOUNTS SCHEDULED: ASSETS	AMOUNTS SCHEDULED: LIABILITIES	AMOUNTS SCHEDULED: OTHER
A - Real Property			$		
B - Personal Property			$		
C - Property Claimed as Exempt					
D - Creditors Holding Secured Claims				$	
E - Creditors Holding Unsecured Priority Claims				$	
F - Creditors Holding Unsecured Non Priority Claims				$	
G - Executory Contracts and Unexpired Leases					
H - Codebtors					
I - Current Income of Individual Debtor(s)					$
J. - Current Expenditures of Individual Debtor(s)					$
Total Number of Sheets of ALL Schedules ->					
		Total Assets ->	$		
			Total Liabilities ->	$	

In re____, Case No.________________________________

Debtor (If known)

SCHEDULE A - REAL PROPERTY

Except as directed below, list all real property in which the debtor has any legal, equitable, or future interest, including all property owned as a co-tenant, community property, or in which the debtor has a life estate. Include any property in which the debtor holds rights and powers exercisable for the debtor's own benefit. If the debtor is married, state whether husband, wife, or both own the property by placing an "H," "W," "J," or "C" in the column labeled "Husband, Wife, Joint, Or Community." If the debtor holds no interest in real property, write "None" under "Description and Location of Property."

Do not include interests in executory contracts and unexpired leases on this schedule. List them in Schedule G - Executory Contracts and Unexpired Leases.

If an entity claims to have a lien or hold a secured interest in any property, state the amount of the secured claim. See Schedule D. If no entity claims to hold a secured interest in the property, write "None" in the column labeled "Amount of Secured Claim."

If the debtor is an individual or if a joint petition is filed, state the amount of any exemption claimed in the property only in Schedule C - Property Claimed as Exempt.

DESCRIPTION AND LOCATION OF PROPERTY	NATURE OF DEBTOR'S INTEREST IN PROPERTY	HUSBAND, WIFE, JOINT OR COMMUNITY	CURRENT MARKET VALUE OF DEBTOR'S INTEREST IN PROPERTY, WITHOUT DEDUCTING ANY SECURED CLAIM OR EXEMPTION	AMOUNT OF SECURED CLAIM
		Total ->	$	

(Report also on Summary of Schedules.)

In re_______________________________________, Case No.______________________________

Debtor (If known)

SCHEDULE B - PERSONAL PROPERTY

Except as directed below, list all personal property of the debtor of whatever kind. If the debtor has no property in one or more of the categories, place an "X" in the appropriate position in the column labeled "None." If additional space is needed in any category, attach a separate sheet properly identified with the case name, and the number of the category. If the debtor is married, state whether husband, wife, or both own the property by placing an "H," "W," "J," or "C" in the column labeled "Husband, Wife, Joint, or Community." If the debtor is an individual or a joint petition is filed, state the amount of any exemptions claimed only in Schedule C - Property Claimed as Exempt.

Do not list interests in executory contracts and unexpired leases on this schedule. List them in Schedule G - Executory Contracts and Unexpired Leases.

If the property is being held for the debtor by someone else, state that person's name and address under "Description and Location of Property."

TYPE OF PROPERTY	NONE	DESCRIPTION AND LOCATION OF PROPERTY	HUSBAND, WIFE, JOINT OR COMMUNITY	CURRENT MARKET VALUE OF DEBTOR'S INTEREST IN PROPERTY, WITH-OUT DEDUCTING ANY SECURED CLAIM OR EXEMPTION
1. Cash on hand.				
2. Checking, savings or other financial accounts, certificates of deposit, or shares in banks, savings and loan, thrift, building and loan, and homestead associations, or credit unions, brokerage houses, or cooperatives.				
3. Security deposits with public utilities, telephone companies, landlords, and others.				
4. Household goods and furnishings, including audio, video, and computer equipment.				
5. Books; pictures and other art objects; antiques; stamp, coin, record, tape, compact disc, and other collections or collectibles.				
6. Wearing apparel.				
7. Furs and jewelry.				
8. Firearms and sports, photographic, and other hobby equipment.				
9. Interests in insurance policies. Name insurance company of each policy and itemize surrender or refund value of each.				
10. Annuities. Itemize and name each issuer.				

In re____, Case No._______________________________________

Debtor (If known)

SCHEDULE B - PERSONAL PROPERTY
(Continuation Sheet)

TYPE OF PROPERTY	NONE	DESCRIPTION AND LOCATION OF PROPERTY	HUSBAND, WIFE, JOINT OR COMMUNITY	CURRENT MARKET VALUE OF DEBTOR'S INTEREST IN PROPERTY, WITHOUT DEDUCTING ANY SECURED CLAIM OR EXEMPTION
11. Interests in IRA, ERISA, Keogh, or other pension or profit sharing Plans. Itemize.				
12. Stock and interests in incorporated and unincorporated businesses. Itemize.				
13. Interests in partnerships or joint ventures. Itemize.				
14. Government and corporate bonds and other negotiable and nonnegotiable instruments.				
15. Accounts Receivable.				
16. Alimony, maintenance, support, and property settlements to which the debtor is or may be entitled. Give particulars.				
17. Other liquidated debts owing debtor including tax refunds. Give particulars.				
18. Equitable or future interests, life estates, and rights or powers exercisable for the benefit of the debtor other than those listed in Schedule of Real Property.				
19. Contingent and non-contingent interests in estate of a decedent, death benefit plan, life insurance policy, or trust.				
20. Other contingent and unliquidated claims of every nature, including tax refunds, counterclaims of the debtor, and rights to setoff claims. Give estimated value of each.				
21. Patents, copyrights, and other intellectual property. Give particulars.				
22. Licenses, franchises, and other general intangibles. Give particulars.				

In re__________________________________, Case No.____________________________
Debtor (If known)

SCHEDULE B - PERSONAL PROPERTY
(Continuation Sheet)

TYPE OF PROPERTY	NONE	DESCRIPTION AND LOCATION OF PROPERTY	HUSBAND, WIFE, JOINT OR COMMUNITY	CURRENT MARKET VALUE OF DEBTOR'S INTEREST IN PROPERTY, WITHOUT DEDUCTING ANY SECURED CLAIM OR EXEMPTION
23. Automobiles, trucks, trailers, and other vehicles and accessories.				
24. Boats, motors, and accessories.				
25. Aircraft and accessories.				
26. Office equipment, furnishings, and supplies.				
27. Machinery, fixtures, equipment, and supplies used in business.				
28. Inventory.				
29. Animals.				
30. Crops - growing or harvested. Give particulars.				
31. Farming equipment and implements.				
32. Farm supplies, chemicals, and feed.				
33. Other personal property of any kind not already listed. Itemize.				

______ continuation sheets attached **Total ->** $

(Include amounts from any continuation sheets attached. Report total also on Summary of Schedules.)

In re____, Case No.____

Debtor (If known)

SCHEDULE C - PROPERTY CLAIMED AS EXEMPT

Debtor elects the exemptions to which debtor is entitled under:

(Check one box)

☐ 11 U.S.C. § 522(b)(1): Exemptions provided in 11 U.S.C. § 522(d). **Note: These exemptions are available only in certain states.**

☐ 11 U.S.C. § 522(b)(2): Exemptions available under applicable nonbankruptcy federal laws, state or local law where the debtor's domicile has been located for the 180 days immediately preceding the filing of the petition, or for a longer portion of the 180-day period than in any other place, and the debtor's interest as a tenant by the entirety or joint tenant to the extent the interest is exempt from process under applicable nonbankruptcy law.

DESCRIPTION OF PROPERTY	SPECIFY LAW PROVIDING EACH EXEMPTION	VALUE OF CLAIMED EXEMPTION	CURRENT MARKET VALUE OF PROPERTY WITHOUT DEDUCTING EXEMPTION

In re______________________________, Case No.______________________________

Debtor (If known)

SCHEDULE D - CREDITORS HOLDING SECURED CLAIMS

State the name, mailing address, including zip code, and account number, if any, of all entities holding claims secured by property of the debtor as of the date of filing of the petition. List creditors holding all types of secured interests such as judgment liens, garnishments, statutory liens, mortgages, deeds of trust, and other security interests. List creditors in alphabetical order to the extent practicable. If all secured creditors will not fit on this page, use the continuation sheet provided.

If any entity other than a spouse in a joint case may be jointly liable on a claim, place an "X" in the column labeled "Codebtor," include the entity on the appropriate schedule of creditors, and complete Schedule H - Codebtors. If a joint petition is filed, state whether husband, wife, both of them, or the marital community may be liable on each claim by placing an "H," "W," "J," or "C" in the column labeled "Husband, Wife, Joint, or Community."

If the claim is contingent, place an "X" in the column labeled "Contingent." If the claim is unliquidated, place an "X" in the column labeled "Unliquidated." If the claim is disputed, place an "X" in the column labeled "Disputed." (You may need to place an "X" in more than one of these three columns.)

Report the total of all claims listed on this schedule in the box labeled "Total" on the last sheet of the completed schedule. Report this total also on the Summary of Schedules.

☐ Check this box if debtor has no creditors holding secured claims to report on this Schedule D.

CREDITOR'S NAME AND MAILING ADDRESS INCLUDING ZIP CODE	CODEBTOR	HUSBAND, WIFE, JOINT OR COMMUNITY	DATE CLAIM WAS INCURRED, NATURE OF LIEN, AND DESCRIPTION AND MARKET VALUE OF PROPERTY SUBJECT TO LIEN	CONTINGENT	UNLIQUIDATED	DISPUTED	AMOUNT OF CLAIM WITHOUT DEDUCTING VALUE OF COLLATERAL	UNSECURED PORTION, IF ANY
ACCOUNT NO.			VALUE $					
ACCOUNT NO.			VALUE $					
ACCOUNT NO.			VALUE $					
ACCOUNT NO.			VALUE $					
						Subtotal -> (Total of this page)	$	
						Total -> (Use only on last page)	$	

_______ continuation sheets attached

(Report total also on Summary of Schedules)

In re______________________________________, Case No.______________________
Debtor (If known)

SCHEDULE D - CREDITORS HOLDING SECURED CLAIMS
(Continuation Sheet)

CREDITOR'S NAME AND MAILING ADDRESS INCLUDING ZIP CODE	CODEBTOR	HUSBAND, WIFE, JOINT OR COMMUNITY	DATE CLAIM WAS INCURRED, NATURE OF LIEN, AND DESCRIPTION AND MARKET VALUE OF PROPERTY SUBJECT TO LIEN	CONTINGENT	UNLIQUIDATED	DISPUTED	AMOUNT OF CLAIM WITHOUT DEDUCTING VALUE OF COLLATERAL	UNSECURED PORTION, IF ANY
ACCOUNT NO.								
			VALUE $					
ACCOUNT NO.								
			VALUE $					
ACCOUNT NO.								
			VALUE $					
ACCOUNT NO.								
			VALUE $					
ACCOUNT NO.								
			VALUE $					

Sheet no.____of____continuation sheets attached to Schedule of Creditors Holding Secured Claims

Subtotal -> (Total of this page)	$
Total -> (Use only on last page)	$

(Report total also on Summary of Schedules)

In re: ____, Case No.______________________________

Debtor(s) (if known)

SCHEDULE E - CREDITORS HOLDING UNSECURED PRIORITY CLAIMS

☐ Check this box if debtor has no creditors holding unsecured claims to report on this Schedule E.

TYPE OF PRIORITY CLAIMS (Check the appropriate box(es) below if claims in that category are listed on the attached sheets)

☐ **Extensions of credit in an involuntary case** Claims arising in the ordinary course of the debtor's business or financial affairs after the commencement of the case but before the earlier of the appointment of a trustee or the order for relief. 11 U.S.C. §507 (a)(2).

☐ **Wages, salaries, and commissions** Wages, salaries, and commissions, including vacation, severance, and sick leave pay owing to employees, and commissions owing to qualifying independent sales representatives up to $4,000* per person, earned within 90 days immediately preceding the filing of the original petition or the cessation of business, whichever occurred first, to the extent provided in 11 U.S.C. §507 (a)(3).

☐ **Contributions to employee benefit plans** Money owed to employee benefit plans for services rendered within 180 days immediately preceding the filing of the original petition or the cessation of business, whichever occurred first, to the extent provided in 11 U.S.C. §507 (a)(4).

☐ **Certain farmers and fishermen** Claims of certain farmers and fishermen, up to $4,000* per farmer or fisherman, against the debtor, as provided in 11 U.S.C. § 507 (a)(5).

☐ **Deposits by individuals** Claims of individuals up to $1,800* for deposits for the purchase, lease, or rental of property or services for personal, family, or household use that were not delivered or provided. 11 U.S.C. §507 (a)(6).

☐ **Alimony, Maintenance, or Support** Claims of a spouse, former spouse, or child of the debtor for alimony, maintenance, or support, to the extent provided in 11 U.S.C. §507 (a)(7).

☐ **Taxes and Certain Other Debts Owed to Governmental Units** Taxes, customs duties, and penalties owing to federal, state, and local governmental units as set forth in 11 U.S.C. §507 (a)(8).

☐ **Commitments to Maintain the Capital of an Insured Depository Institution** Claims based on commitments to the FDIC, RTC, Director of the Office of Thrift Supervision, Comptroller of the Currency, or Board of Governors of the Federal Reserve System, or their predecessors or successors, to maintain the capital of an insured depository institution. 11 U.S.C. §507 (a)(9).

✷ Amounts are subject to adjustment on April 1, 1998, and every three years thereafter with respect to cases commenced on or after the date of adjustment.

CREDITOR'S NAME AND MAILING ADDRESS INCLUDING ZIP CODE	CODEBT	HWJC	DATE CLAIM WAS INCURRED AND CONSIDERATION FOR CLAIM	CUD*	TOTAL AMOUNT OF CLAIM	AMOUNT ENTITLED TO PRIORITY
A/C#						
A/C#						
A/C#						
A/C#						
A/C#						

________ Continuation sheets attached.

Subtotal -> (Total of this page) $

Total -> (use only on last page of the completed Schedule E) $

*If contingent, enter C; if unliquidated, enter U; if disputed, enter D.

(Report total also on Summary of Schedules)

In re ______________________________, Case No. ______________________
Debtor (If known)

SCHEDULE E - CREDITORS HOLDING UNSECURED PRIORITY CLAIMS
(Continuation sheet)

____
TYPE OF PRIORITY

CREDITOR'S NAME AND MAILING ADDRESS INCLUDING ZIP CODE	CODEBTOR	HUSBAND, WIFE, JOINT OR COMMUNITY	DATE CLAIM WAS INCURRED AND CONSIDERATION	CONTINGENT	UNLIQUIDATED	DISPUTED	TOTAL AMOUNT OF CLAIM	AMOUNT ENTITLED TO PRIORITY
ACCOUNT NO.								
ACCOUNT NO.								
ACCOUNT NO.								
ACCOUNT NO.								
ACCOUNT NO.								

Sheet no.______of______sheets attached to Schedule of Creditors Holding Unsecured Priority Claims

Subtotal -> (Total of this page) $

Total -> (Use only on last page of the completed Schedule E.) $

(Report total also on Summary of Schedules)

In re____, Case No.________________________________
Debtor (If Known)

SCHEDULE F - CREDITORS HOLDING UNSECURED NONPRIORITY CLAIMS

State the name, mailing address, including zip code, and account number, if any, of all entities holding unsecured claims without priority against the debtor or the property of the debtor, as of the date of filing of the petition. Do not include claims listed in Schedules D and E. If all creditors will not fit on this page, use the continuation sheet provided.

If any entity other than a spouse in a joint case may be jointly liable on a claim, place an"X" in the column labeled "Codebtor," include the entity on the appropriate schedule of creditors, and complete Schedule H - Codebtors. If a joint petition is filed, state whether husband, wife, both of them, or the marital community may be liable on each claim by placing an "H," "W," "J," or "C" in the column labeled "Husband, Wife, Joint, or Community."

If the claim is contingent, place an "X" in the column labeled "Contigent." If the claim is unliquidated, place an"X" in the column labeled "Unliquidated." If the claim is disputed, place an "X" in the column labeled "Disputed." (You may need to place an"X" in more than one of these three columns.)

Report total of all claims listed on this schedule in the box labeled "Total" on the last sheet of the completed schedule. Report this total also on the Summary of Schedules.

☐ Check this box if debtor has no creditors holding unsecured nonpriority claims to report on this Schedule F.

CREDITOR'S NAME AND MAILING ADDRESS INCLUDING ZIP CODE	CODEBTOR	HUSBAND, WIFE, JOINT OR COMMUNITY	DATE CLAIM WAS INCURRED AND CONSIDERATION FOR CLAIM. IF CLAIM IS SUBJECT TO SETOFF, SO STATE	CONTINGENT	UNLIQUIDATED	DISPUTED	AMOUNT OF CLAIM
ACCOUNT NO.							
ACCOUNT NO.							
ACCOUNT NO.							
ACCOUNT NO.							

_______ Continuation sheets attached

Subtotal - > (Total of this page)	$
Total - > (Use only on last page of the completed Schedule F)	$

(Report total also on Summary of Schedules)

In re ______________________________, Case No. ______________________________
(Debtor) (If known)

SCHEDULE F - CREDITORS HOLDING UNSECURED NONPRIORITY CLAIMS

(Continuation Sheet)

CREDITOR'S NAME AND MAILING ADDRESS INCLUDING ZIP CODE	CODEBTOR	HUSBAND,WIFE,JOINT OR COMMUNITY	DATE CLAIM WAS INCURRED AND CONSIDERATION FOR CLAIM. IF CLAIM IS SUBJECT TO SETOFF, SO STATE	CONTINGENT	UNLIQUIDATED	DISPUTED	AMOUNT OF CLAIM
ACCOUNT NO.							
ACCOUNT NO.							
ACCOUNT NO.							
ACCOUNT NO.							
ACCOUNT NO.							

Sheet no. _____ of _____ sheets attached to Schedule of Creditors Holding Unsecured Nonpriority Claims

Subtotal - > (Total of this page)	$
Total - > (Use only on last page of the completed Schedule F)	$

(Report total also on Summary of Schedule)

In re____, Case No.______________________________________
Debtor (If known)

SCHEDULE G. EXECUTORY CONTRACTS AND UNEXPIRED LEASES

Describe all executory contracts of any nature and all unexpired leases of real or personal property. Include any timeshare interests.

State nature of debtor's interest in contract, i.e., "Purchaser," "Agent," etc. State whether debtor is the lessor or lessee of a lease.

Provide the names and complete mailing addresses of all other parties to each lease or contract described.

NOTE: A party listed on this schedule will not receive notice of the filing of this case unless the party is also scheduled in the appropriate schedule of creditors.

☐ Check this box if debtor has no executory contracts or unexpired leases.

NAME AND MAILING ADDRESS, INCLUDING ZIP CODE, OF OTHER PARTIES TO LEASE OR CONTRACT.	DESCRIPTION OF CONTRACT OR LEASE AND NATURE OF DEBTOR'S INTEREST. STATE WHETHER LEASE IS FOR NONRESIDENTIAL REAL PROPERTY. STATE CONTRACT NUMBER OF ANY GOVERNMENT CONTRACT.

In re____, Case No.____________________________
Debtor (If known)

SCHEDULE H - CODEBTORS

Provide the information requested concerning any person or entity, other than a spouse in a joint case, that is also liable on any debts listed by debtor in the schedules of creditors. Include all guarantors and co-signers. In community property states, a married debtor not filing a joint case should report the name and address of the nondebtor spouse on this schedule. Include all names used by the nondebtor spouse during the six years immediately preceding the commencement of this case.

☐ Check this box if debtor has no codebtors.

NAME AND ADDRESS OF CODEBTOR	NAME AND ADDRESS OF CREDITOR

In re______________________________________, Case No.______________________________
Debtor (If known)

SCHEDULE I - CURRENT INCOME OF INDIVIDUAL DEBTOR(S)

The column labeled "Spouse" must be completed in all cases filed by joint debtors and by a married debtor in a chapter 12 or 13 case whether or not a joint petition is filed, unless the spouses are separated and a joint petition is not filed.

Debtor's Marital Status:	DEPENDENTS OF DEBTOR AND SPOUSE		
	NAMES	AGE	RELATIONSHIP

Employment:	DEBTOR	SPOUSE
Occupation		
Name of Employer		
How long employed		
Address of Employer		

Income: (Estimate of average monthly income)	DEBTOR	SPOUSE
Current monthly gross wages, salary, and commissions (prorate if not paid monthly.)	$________	$________
Estimated monthly overtime	$________	$________
SUBTOTAL	$________	$________
LESS PAYROLL DEDUCTIONS		
a. Payroll taxes and social security	$________	$________
b. Insurance	$________	$________
c. Union dues	$________	$________
d. Other (Specify:________________________)	$________	$________
SUBTOTAL OF PAYROLL DEDUCTIONS	$________	$________
TOTAL NET MONTHLY TAKE HOME PAY	$________	$________
Regular income from operation of business or profession or farm (attach detailed statement)	$________	$________
Income from real property	$________	$________
Interest and dividends	$________	$________
Alimony, maintenance or support payments payable to the debtor for the debtor's use or that of dependents listed above.	$________	$________
Social security or other government assistance (Specify)________________________	$________	$________
Pension or retirement income	$________	$________
Other monthly income	$________	$________
(Specify)________________________	$________	$________
________________________	$________	$________
TOTAL MONTHLY INCOME	$________	$________

TOTAL COMBINED MONTHLY INCOME $______________ (Report also on Summary of Schedules)

Describe any increase or decrease of more than 10% in any of the above categories anticipated to occur within the year following the filing of this document:

In re ____, Case No. ______________________________
Debtor (If known)

SCHEDULE J- CURRENT EXPENDITURES OF INDIVIDUAL DEBTOR(S)

Complete this schedule by estimating the average monthly expenses of the debtor and the debtor's family. Prorate any payments made bi-weekly, quarterly, semi-annually, or annually to show monthly rate.

☐ Check this box if a joint petition is filed and debtor's spouse maintains a separate household. Complete a separate schedule of expenditures labeled "Spouse."

Rent or home mortgage payment (include lot rented for mobile home)	$____________
Are real estate taxes included? Yes _______ No _______	
Is property insurance included? Yes _______ No _______	
Utilities Electricity and heating fuel	$____________
Water and sewer	$____________
Telephone	$____________
Other ______________________________	$____________
Home maintenance (repairs and upkeep)	$____________
Food	$____________
Clothing	$____________
Laundry and dry cleaning	$____________
Medical and dental expenses	$____________
Transportation (not including car payment)	$____________
Recreation, clubs and entertainment, newspapers, magazines, etc.	$____________
Charitable contributions	$____________
Insurance (not deducted from wages or included in home mortgage payments)	
Homeowner's or renter's	$____________
Life	$____________
Health	$____________
Auto	$____________
Other ______________________________	$____________
Taxes (not deducted from wages or included in home mortgage payments)	
(Specify)______________________________	$____________
Installment payments: (in Chapter 12 and 13 cases, do not list payments to be included in the plan)	
Auto	$____________
Other______________________________	$____________
Other______________________________	$____________
Alimony, maintenance, and support paid to others	$____________
Payments for support of additional dependents not living at your home	$____________
Regular expenses from operation of business, profession, or farm (attach detailed statement)	$____________
Other______________________________	$____________
TOTAL MONTHLY EXPENSES (Report also on Summary of Schedules)	$____________

[FOR CHAPTER 12 AND 13 DEBTORS ONLY]

Provide the information requested below, including whether plan payments are to be made bi-weekly, monthly, annually, or at some other regular interval.

A. Total projected monthly income	$____________
B. Total projected monthly expenses	$____________
C. Excess income (A minus B)	$____________
D. Total amount to be paid into plan each ______________________ (interval)	$____________

In re ____, Case No. ________________________________
Debtor (If known)

DECLARATION CONCERNING DEBTOR'S SCHEDULES

DECLARATION UNDER PENALTY OF PERJURY BY INDIVIDUAL DEBTOR

I declare under penalty of perjury that I have read the foregoing summary and schedules, consisting of ______ sheets and that they are true and correct to the best of my knowledge, information, and belief. (Total shown on summary page plus 1)

Date ________________________________ Signature: ________________________________
Debtor

Date ________________________________ Signature: ________________________________
(Joint Debtor, if any)
(If joint case, both spouses must sign.)

CERTIFICATION AND SIGNATURE OF NON-ATTORNEY BANKRUPTCY PETITION PREPARER (See 11 U.S.C. § 110)

I certify that I am a bankruptcy petition preparer as defined in 11 U.S.C. § 110, that I have prepared this document for compensation, and that I have provided the debtor with a copy of this document.

________________________________ ________________________________
Printed or Typed Name of Bankruptcy Petition Preparer Social Security Number

____

____
Address

Names and Social Security Numbers of all other individuals who prepared or assisted in preparing this document:

If more than one person prepared this document, attach additional signed sheets conforming to the appropriate Official Form for each person.

X________________________________ ________________________________
Signature of Bankruptcy Petition Preparer Date

A bankruptcy petition preparer's failure to comply with the provisions of Title 11 and the Federal Rules of Bankruptcy Procedure may result in fines or imprisonment or both. 11 U.S.C. § 110; 18 U.S.C. § 156.

DECLARATION UNDER PENALTY OF PERJURY ON BEHALF OF CORPORATION OR PARTNERSHIP

I, the ______________________________ [president or other officer or an authorized agent of the corporation or a member or an authorized agent of the partnership] of the ______________________________ [corporation or partnership] named as debtor in this case, declare under penalty of perjury that I have read the foregoing summary and schedules, consisting of ______________________ sheets (total shown on summary page plus 1), and that they are true and correct to the best of my knowledge, information, and belief.

Date ________________________________

Signature: ________________________________

____
[Print or type name of individual signing on behalf of debtor.]

[An individual signing on behalf of a partnership or corporation must indicate position or relationship to debtor.]

Penalty for making a false statement or concealing property: Fine of up to $500,000 or imprisonment for up to 5 years or both. 18 U.S.C. § 152 and 3571.

UNITED STATES BANKRUPTCY COURT
______________DISTRICT OF______________

In re: ______________________________, Case No. ______________________
Debtor (if known)

STATEMENT OF FINANCIAL AFFAIRS

This statement is to be completed by every debtor. Spouses filing a joint petition may file a single statement on which the information for both spouses is combined. If the case is filed under Chapter 12 or Chapter 13, a married debtor must furnish information for both spouses whether or not a joint petition is filed, unless the spouses are separated and a joint petition is not filed. An individual debtor engaged in business as a sole proprietor, partner, family farmer, or self-employed professional should provide the information requested on this statement concerning all such activities as well as the individual's personal affairs.

Questions 1-15 are to be completed by all debtors. Debtors that are or have been in business, as defined below, also must complete Questions 16-21. **Each question must be answered. If the answer to any question is "None," or the question is not applicable, mark the box labeled "None."** If additional space is needed for the answer to any question, use and attach a separate sheet properly identified with the case name, case number (if known), and the number of the question.

DEFINITIONS

In business - A debtor is "in business" for the purpose of this form if the debtor is a corporation or partnership. An individual debtor is "in business" for the purpose of this form if the debtor is or has been, within the two years immediately preceding the filing of this bankruptcy case, any of the following: an officer, director, managing executive, or person in control of a corporation; a partner, other than a limited partner, of a partnership; a sole proprietor or self-employed.

Insider - The term "insider" includes but is not limited to: relatives of the debtor; general partners of the debtor and their relatives; corporations of which the debtor is an officer, director, or person in control; officers, directors, and any person in control of a corporate debtor and their relatives; affiliates of the debtor and insiders of such affiliates; any managing agent of the debtor. 11 U.S.C.§ 101(30).

---

1. Income from employment or operation of business

None ☐ State the gross amount of income the debtor has received from employment, trade, or profession, or from operation of the debtor's business from the beginning of this calendar year to the date this case was commenced. State also the gross amounts received during the two years immediately preceding this calendar year. (A debtor that maintains, or has maintained, financial records on the basis of a fiscal rather than a calendar year may report fiscal year income. Identify the beginning and ending dates of the debtor's fiscal year.) If a joint petition is filed, state income for each spouse separately. (Married debtors filing under Chapter 12 or Chapter 13 must state income of both spouses whether or not a joint petition is filed, unless the spouses are separated and a joint petition is not filed.)

Amount Source (if more than one)

2. Income other than from employment or operation of business

None ☐

State the amount of income received by the debtor other than from employment, trade, profession, or operation of the debtor's business during the **two years** immediately preceding the commencement of this case. Give particulars. If a joint petition is filed, state income for each spouse separately. (Married debtors filing under Chapter 12 or Chapter 13 must state income for each spouse whether or not a joint petition is filed, unless the spouses are separated and a joint petition is not filed.)

Amount	Source

3. Payments to creditors

None ☐

a. List all payments on loans, installment purchases of goods or services, and other debts, aggregating more than $600 to any creditor, made within **90 days** immediately preceding the commencement of this case. (Married debtors filing under Chapter 12 or Chapter 13 must include payments by either or both spouses whether or not a joint petition is filed, unless the spouses are separated and a joint petition is not filed.)

Names and addresses of creditors	Dates of payments	Amount paid	Amount still owing

None ☐

b. List all payments made within **one year** immediately preceding the commencement of this case to or for the benefit of creditors who are or were insiders. (Married debtors filing under Chapter 12 or Chapter 13 must include payments by either or both spouses whether or not a joint petition is filed, unless the spouses are separated and a joint petition is not filed.)

Name and address of creditor and relationship of debtor	Date of payment	Amount paid	Amount still owing

4. Suits, executions, garnishments and attachments

None ☐

a. List all suits to which the debtor is or was a party within **one year** immediately preceding the filing of this case. (Married debtors filing under Chapter 12 or Chapter 13 must include information concerning either or both spouses whether or not a joint petition is filed, unless the spouses are separated and a joint petition is not filed.)

Caption of suit and case number	Nature of proceeding	Court and location	Status or disposition

None

☐

b. Describe all property that has been attached, garnished or seized under any legal or equitable process within **one year** immediately preceding the commencement of this case. (Married debtors filing under Chapter 12 or Chapter 13 must include information concerning property of either or both spouses whether or not a joint petition is filed, unless the spouses are separated and a joint petition is not filed.)

Name and address of person for whose benefit property was seized	Date of seizure	Description and value of property

None

☐

5. Repossessions, foreclosures and returns

List all property that has been repossessed by a creditor, sold at a foreclosure sale, transferred through a deed in lieu of foreclosure or returned to the seller within **one year** immediately preceding the commencement of this case. (Married debtors filing under Chapter 12 or Chapter 13 must include information concerning property of either or both spouses whether or not a joint petition is filed, unless the spouses are separated and a joint petition is not filed.)

Name and address of creditor or seller	Date of repossession, foreclosure sale, transfer or return	Description and value of property

None

☐

6. Assignments and receiverships

a. Describe any assignment of property for the benefit of creditors made within **120 days** immediately preceding the commencement of this case. (Married debtors filing under Chapter 12 or Chapter 13 must include any assignment by either or both spouses whether or not a joint petition is filed, unless the spouses are separated and a joint petition is not filed.)

Name and address of assignee	Date of assignment	Terms of assignment or settlement

None

☐

b. List all property which has been in the hands of a custodian, receiver, or court-appointed official within **one year** immediately preceding the commencement of this case. (Married debtors filing under Chapter 12 or Chapter 13 must include information concerning property of either or both spouses whether or not a joint petition is filed, unless the spouses are separated and a joint petition is not filed.)

Name and address of custodian	Name and location of court	Case title and number	Date of order	Description and value of property

7. Gifts

None

☐ List all gifts or charitable contributions made within **one year** immediately preceding the commencement of this case except ordinary and usual gifts to family members aggregating less than $200 in value per individual family member, and charitable contributions aggregating less than $100 per recipient. (Married debtors filing under Chapter 12 or Chapter 13 must include gifts or contributions by either or both spouses whether or not a joint petition is filed, unless the spouses are separated and a joint petition is not filed.)

Name and address of person or organization	Relationship to debtor, if any	Date of gift	Description and value of gift

8. Losses

None

☐ List all losses from fire, theft, other casualty or gambling within **one year** immediately preceding the commencement of this case **or since the commencement of this case.** (Married debtors filing under Chapter 12 or Chapter 13 must include losses by either or both spouses whether or not a joint petition is filed, unless the spouses are separated and a joint petition is not filed.)

Description and value of property	Description of circumstances and, if loss was covered in whole or in part by insurance, give particulars	Date of loss

9. Payments related to debt counseling or bankruptcy

None

☐ List all payments made or property transferred by or on behalf of the debtor to any persons, including attorneys, for consultation concerning debt consolidation, relief under the bankruptcy law or preparation of a petition in bankruptcy within **one year** immediately preceding the commencement of this case.

Name and address of payee	Date of payment	Name of payor if other than debtor	Amount of money or description and value of property

10. Other transfers

None ☐ **a.** List all other property, other than property transferred in the ordinary course of the business or financial affairs of the debtor, transferred either absolutely or as security within **one year** immediately preceding the commencement of this case. (Married debtors filing under Chapter 12 or Chapter 13 must include transfers by either or both spouses whether or not a joint petition is filed, unless the spouses are separated and a joint petition is not filed.)

Name and address of transferee	Relationship to debtor	Transfer date	Property transferred and value received

11. Closed financial accounts

None ☐ List all financial accounts and instruments held in the name of the debtor or for the benefit of the debtor that were closed, sold, or otherwise transferred within **one year** immediately preceding the commencement of this case. Include checking, savings, or other financial accounts, certificates of deposit, or other instruments; shares and share accounts held in banks, credit unions, pension funds, cooperatives, associations, brokerage houses and other financial institutions. (Married debtors filing under Chapter 12 or Chapter 13 must include information concerning accounts or instruments held by or for either or both spouses whether or not a joint petition is filed, unless the spouses are separated and a joint petition is not filed.)

Name and address of institution	Type and number of account and final balance	Amount and rate of sale or closing

12. Safe deposit boxes

None ☐ List each safe deposit or other box or depository in which the debtor has or had securities, cash, or other valuables within **one year** immediately preceding the commencement of this case. (Married debtors filing under Chapter 12 or Chapter 13 must include boxes or depositories of either or both spouses whether or not a joint petition is filed, unless the spouses are separated and a joint petition is not filed.)

Name and address of bank or other depository	Name and addresses of those with access to box or depository	Description of contents	Date of transfer or surrender, if any

13. Setoffs

None ☐ List all setoffs made by any creditor, including a bank, against a debt or deposit of the debtor within **90 days** preceding the commencement of this case. (Married debtors filing under Chapter 12 or Chapter 13 must include information concerning either or both spouses whether or not a joint petition is filed, unless the spouses are separated and a joint petition is not filed.)

Name and address of creditor	Date of setoff	Amount of setoff

14. Property held for another person

None ☐ List all property owned by another person that the debtor holds or controls.

Name and address of owner	Description and value of property	Location of property

15. Prior address of debtor

None ☐ If the debtor has moved within the **two years** immediately preceding the commencement of this case, list all premises which the debtor occupied during that period and vacated prior to the commencement of this case. If a joint petition is filed, report also any separate address of either spouse.

Address	Name used	Dates of occupancy

The following questions are to be completed by every debtor that is a corporation or partnership and by any individual debtor who is or has been, within the **two years** immediately preceding the commencement of this case, any of the following: an officer, director, managing executive, or owner of more than 5 percent of the voting securities of a corporation; a partner, other than a limited partner, of a partnership; a sole proprietor or otherwise self-employed.

(An individual or joint debtor should complete this portion of the statement **only** *if the debtor is or has been in business, as defined above, within the* **two years** *immediately preceding the commencement of this case.)*

16. Nature, location and name of business

None ☐ **a.** If the debtor is an individual, list the names and addresses of all businesses in which the debtor was an officer, director, partner, or managing executive of a corporation, partnership, sole proprietorship, or was a self-employed professional within the **two years** immediately preceding the commencement of this case, or in which the debtor owned 5 percent or more of the voting or equity securities within the **two years** immediately preceding the commencement of this case.

b. If the debtor is a partnership, list the names and addresses of all businesses in which the debtor was a partner or owned 5 percent or more of the voting securities within the **two years** immediately preceding the commencement of this case.

c. If the debtor is a corporation, list the names and addresses of all businesses in which the debtor was a partner or owned 5 percent or more of the voting securities within the **two years** immediately preceding the commencement of this case.

Name	Address	Nature of business	Beginning and ending Dates of operation

17. Books, records and financial statements

None ☐ **a.** List all bookkeepers and accountants who within the **six years** immediately preceding the filing of this bankruptcy case kept or supervised the keeping of books of account and records of the debtor.

Name	Address	Dates services rendered

None ☐ **b.** List all firms or individuals who within the **two years** immediately preceding the filing of this bankruptcy case have audited the books of account and records, or prepared a financial statement of the debtor.

Name	Address	Dates services rendered

None

☐ **c.** List all firms or individuals who at the time of the commencement of this case were in possession of the books of account and records of the debtor. If any of the books of account and records are not available, please explain.

Name	Address

None

☐ **d.** List all financial institutions, creditors and other parties, including mercantile and trade agencies, to whom a financial statement was issued within the **two years** immediately preceding the commencement of this case by the debtor.

Name	Address	Date issued

18. Inventories

None

☐ **a.** List the dates of the **last two** inventories taken of your property, the name of the person who supervised the taking of each inventory, and the dollar amount and basis of each inventory.

Date of inventory	Inventory supervisor	Dollar amount of inventory (Specify cost, market or other basis)

None

☐ **b.** List the name and address of the person having possession of the records of each of the two inventories reported in a., above.

Date of inventory	Name and addresses of custodian of inventory records

19. Current partners, officers, directors and shareholders

None

☐ **a.** If the debtor is a partnership, list the nature and percentage of partnership interest of each member of the partnership.

Name and address	Nature of interest	Percentage of interest

None ☐ b. If the debtor is a corporation, list all officers and directors of the corporation, and each stockholder who directly or indirectly owns, controls, or holds 5 percent or more of the voting securities of the corporation.

Name and address	Title	Nature and percentage of stock ownership

20. Former partners, officers, directors and shareholders

None ☐ **a.** If the debtor is a partnership, list each member who withdrew from the partnership within **one year** immediately preceding the commencement of this case.

Name	Address	Date of withdrawal

None ☐ **b.** If the debtor is a corporation, list all officers or directors whose relationship with the corporation terminated within **one year** immediately preceding the commencement of this case.

Name and address	Title	Date of termination

21. Withdrawals from a partnership or distributions by a corporation

None ☐ If the debtor is a partnership or corporation, list all withdrawals or distributions credited or given to an insider, including compensation in any form, bonuses, loans, stock redemptions, options exercised and any other perquisite during **one year** immediately preceding the commencement of this case.

Name and address of recipient	Relationship to debtor	Date and purpose of withdrawal	Amount of money or description and value of property

[If completed by an individual or individual and spouse]

I declare under penalty of perjury that I have read the answers contained in the foregoing statement of financial affairs and any attachments thereto and that they are true and correct.

Date ___________________________ Signature ___________________________
of Debtor

Date ___________________________ Signature ___________________________
of Joint Debtor
(if any)

CERTIFICATION AND SIGNATURE OF NON-ATTORNEY BANKRUPTCY PETITION PREPARER (See 11 U.S.C. § 110)

I certify that I am a bankruptcy petition preparer as defined in 11 U.S.C. § 110, that I prepared this document for compensation, and that I have provided the debtor with a copy of this document.

____
Printed or Typed Name of Bankruptcy Petition Preparer

____
Social Security Number

____

____
Address

Names and Social Security Numbers of all other individuals who prepared or assisted in preparing this document.
If more than one person prepared this document, attach additional signed sheets conforming to the appropriate Official Form for each person.

X____
Signature of Bankruptcy Petition Preparer

____
Date

A bankruptcy petition preparer's failure to comply with the provisions of Title 11 and the Federal Rules of Bankruptcy Procedure may result in fines or imprisonment or both. 11 U.S.C. § 110; 18 U.S.C. § 156.

[If completed on behalf of a partnership or corporation]

I declare under penalty of perjury that I have read the answers contained in the foregoing statement of financial affairs and any attachments thereto and that they are true and correct to the best of my knowledge, information and belief.

Date ________________________ Signature ________________________________

____
Print Name and Title

[An individual signing on behalf of a partnership or corporation must indicate position or relationship to debtor.]

continuation sheets attached

Penalty for making a false statement: Fine of up to $500,000 or imprisonment for up to 5 years, or both. 18 U.S.C. § 152 and 3571.

UNITED STATES BANKRUPTCY COURT
____________ DISTRICT OF ____________

In re ______________________________, Case No. ____________
Debtor

CHAPTER 7 INDIVIDUAL DEBTOR'S STATEMENT OF INTENTION

1. I, the debtor, have filed a schedule of assets and liabilities which includes consumer debts secured by property of the estate.

2. My intention with respect to the property of the estate which secures those consumer debts is as follows:

a. *Property to Be Surrendered.*

Description of Property	Creditor's Name
1. ____________	____________
2. ____________	____________
3. ____________	____________

b. *Property to Be Retained.* [Check applicable statement of debtor's intention concerning reaffirmation, redemption, or lien avoidance.]

Description of Property	Creditor's Name	Debt will be reaffirmed pursuant to § 524(c)	Property is claimed as exempt and will be redeemed pursuant to § 722	Lien will be avoided pursuant to §522(f) and property will be claimed as exempt
1. ____________	________	________	________	________
2. ____________	________	________	________	________
3. ____________	________	________	________	________
4. ____________	________	________	________	________
5. ____________	________	________	________	________

3. I understand that §521(2)(B) of the Bankruptcy Code requires that I perform the above stated intention within 45 days of the filing of this statement with the court, or within such additional time as the court, for cause, within such 45-day period fixes.

Date: ____________

____
Signature of Debtor

CERTIFICATION AND SIGNATURE OF NON-ATTORNEY BANKRUPTCY PETITION PREPARER
(See 11 U.S.C. § 110)

I certify that I am a bankruptcy petition preparer as defined in 11 U.S.C. § 110, that I have prepared this document for compensation, and that I have provided the debtor with a copy of this document.

____
Printed or Typed Name of Bankruptcy Petition Preparer

____
Social Security Number

____

Names and Social Security numbers of all other individuals who prepared or assisted in preparing this document:

____
Address

If more than one person prepared this document, attach additional signed sheets conforming to the appropriate Official Form for each person.

X____
Signature of Bankruptcy Petition Preparer

____
Date

A bankruptcy petition preparer's failure to comply with the provisions of Title 11 and the Federal Rules of Bankruptcy Procedure may result in fines or imprisonment or both. 11 U.S.C. § 110; 18 U.S.C. § 156.

MASTER MAILING LIST

CASE NO.________________

______Labels Sheet_____ of_____

	NOTE: **Do not type directly on the Typing Guide**	

INSTRUCTIONS FOR COMPLETING MASTER MAILING LIST

1. Use black ink only.
2. Check with your local bankruptcy court clerk for any local rules required in filling out this form.
3. Place white sheet of paper in front of the matrix and type required names within bordered area.
4. Use separate master mailing lists for husband and wife if they **do not** list the same creditors on the schedules.
5. The debtor(s) and the attorney must sign the declaration below if required by any local bankruptcy rule.

DECLARATION

I, ____, do hereby certify, under penalty of perjury, that the master mailing list, consisting of _____sheets, is complete, correct and consistent with the debtor's schedules pursuant to Local Bankruptcy Rule ____________.

____
Debtor

____
Spouse

____
Attorney (If Applicable)

NOTE: If the entity filing has 200 or more creditors or equity holders, they should check with the Clerk of the Bankruptcy Court for any special handling requirements.

NOTE: It is recommended that you check with the Clerk of The Bankruptcy Court regarding his or her preference as to how they wish you to do the mailing list. Some require single rows of addresses while others will accept the three across format.

United States Bankruptcy Court

Case Number

_________________ District of _________________

NOTICE OF COMMENCEMENT OF CASE UNDER CHAPTER 7 OF THE BANKRUPTCY CODE.
MEETING OF CREDITORS, AND FIXING OF DATES
(Individual or Joint Debtor No Asset Case)

In re (Name of Debtor)	Address of Debtor	Soc. Sec. / Tax Id. Nos.
	Date Case Filed (or Converted)	
Name and Address of Attorney for Debtor	Name and Address of Trustee	
Telephone Number	Telephone Number	

☐ This is a converted case originally filed under chapter _____ on _________________ (date).

DATE, TIME, AND LOCATION OF MEETING OF CREDITORS

DISCHARGE OF DEBTS

Deadline to File a Complaint Objecting to Discharge of the Debtor or to Determine Dischargeability of Certain Types of Debts:

AT THIS TIME THERE APPEAR TO BE NO ASSETS AVAILABLE FROM WHICH PAYMENT MAY BE MADE TO UNSECURED CREDITORS. DO NOT FILE A PROOF OF CLAIM UNTIL YOU RECEIVE NOTICE TO DO SO.

COMMENCEMENT OF CASE. A petition for liquidation under chapter 7 of the Bankruptcy Code has been filed in this court by or against the person or persons named above as the debtor, and an order for relief has been entered. You will not receive notice of all documents filed in this case. All documents filed with the court, including lists of the debtor's property, debts, and property claimed as exempt are available for inspection at the office of the clerk of the bankruptcy court.

CREDITORS MAY NOT TAKE CERTAIN ACTIONS.A creditor is anyone to whom the debtor owes money or property. Under the Bankruptcy Code, the debtor is granted certain protection against creditors. Common examples of prohibited actions by creditors are contacting the debtor to demand repayment, taking action against the debtor to collect money owed to creditors or to take property of the debtor, and starting or continuing foreclosure actions, repossessions, or wage deductions. If unauthorized actions are taken by a creditor against a debtor, the court may penalize that creditor. A creditor who is considering taking action against the debtor or the property of the debtor should review § 362 of the Bankruptcy Code and may wish to seek legal advice. The staff of the clerk of the bankruptcy court is not permitted to give legal advice.

MEETING OF CREDITORS. The debtor (both husband and wife in a joint case) is required to appear at the meeting of creditors on the date and at the place set forth above for the purpose of being examined under oath. Attendance by creditors at the meeting is welcomed, but not required. At the meeting, the creditors may elect a trustee other than the one named above, elect a committee of creditors, examine the debtor, and transact such other business as may properly come before the meeting. The meeting may be continued or adjourned from time to time by notice at the meeting, without further written notice to creditors.

LIQUIDATION OF THE DEBTOR'S PROPERTY. The trustee will collect the debtor's property and turn any that is not exempt into money. At this time, however, it appears from the schedules of the debtor that there are no assets from which any distribution can be paid to creditors. If at a later date it appears that there are assets from which a distribution may be paid, the creditors will be notified and given an opportunity to file claims.

EXEMPT PROPERTY. Under state and federal law, the debtor is permitted to keep certain money or property as exempt. If a creditor believes that an exemption of money or property is not authorized by law, the creditor may file an objection. An objection must be filed not later than 30 days after the conclusion of the meeting of creditors.

DISCHARGE OF DEBTS. The debtor is seeking a discharge of debts. A discharge means that certain debts are made unenforceable against the debtor personally. Creditors whose claims against the debtor are discharged may never take action against the debtor to collect the discharged debts. If a creditor believes that the debtor should not receive any discharge of debts under § 727 of the Bankruptcy Code or that a debt owed to the creditor is not dischargable under §523(a)(2), (4), or (6) of the Bankruptcy Code, timely action must be taken in the bankruptcy court by the deadline set forth above in the box labeled "Discharge of Debts." Creditors considering taking such action may wish to seek legal advice.

DO NOT FILE A PROOF OF CLAIM UNLESS YOU RECEIVE A COURT NOTICE TO DO SO

Address of the Clerk of the Bankruptcy Court	For the Court:
	Clerk of the Bankruptcy Court
	Date

United States Bankruptcy Court

Case Number

District of _______________ _______________

NOTICE OF COMMENCEMENT OF CASE UNDER CHAPTER 11 OF THE BANKRUPTCY CODE, MEETING OF CREDITORS, AND FIXING OF DATES
(Individual or Joint Debtor Case)

In re (Name of Debtor)	Address of Debtor	Soc. Sec. / Tax Id. Nos.
	Date Case Filed (or Converted)	
Name and Address of Attorney for Debtor	Name and Address of Trustee	
Telephone Number		Telephone Number

☐ This is a converted case originally filed under chapter ______ on ______________________ (date).

DATE, TIME, AND LOCATION OF MEETING OF CREDITORS

DISCHARGE OF DEBTS

Deadline to File a Complaint to Determine Dischargeability of Certain Types of Debts:

COMMENCEMENT OF CASE. A petition for reorganization under chapter 11 of the Bankruptcy Code has been filed in this court by or against the person or persons named above as the debtor, and an order for relief has been entered. You will not receive notice of all documents filed in this case. All documents filed with the court, including lists of the debtor's property, debts, and property claimed as exempt are available for inspection at the office of the clerk of the bankruptcy court.

CREDITORS MAY NOT TAKE CERTAIN ACTIONS. A creditor is anyone to whom the debtor owes money or property. Under the Bankruptcy Code, the debtor is granted certain protection against creditors. Common examples of prohibited actions by creditors are contacting the debtor to demand repayment, taking action against the debtor to collect money owed to creditors or to take property of the debtor, and starting or continuing foreclosure actions, repossessions, or wage deductions. If unauthorized actions are taken by a creditor against a debtor , the court may penalize that creditor. A creditor who is considering taking action against the debtor or the property of the debtor should review § 362 of the Bankruptcy Code and may wish to seek legal advice. The staff of the clerk of the bankruptcy court is not permitted to give legal advice.

MEETING OF CREDITORS. The debtor (both husband and wife in a joint case) is required to appear at the meeting of creditors on the date and at the place set forth above for the purpose of being examined under oath. Attendance by creditors at the meeting is welcomed, but not required. At the meeting, the creditors may examine the debtor and transact such other business as may properly come before the meeting. The meeting may be continued or adjourned from time to time by notice at the meeting, without further written notice to creditors.

EXEMPT PROPERTY. Under state and federal law, the debtor is permitted to keep certain money or property as exempt. If a creditor believes that an exemption of money or property is not authorized by law, the creditor may file an objection. An objection must be filed not later than 30 days after the conclusion of the meeting of creditors.

DISCHARGE OF DEBTS. The debtor may seek a discharge of debts. A discharge means that certain debts are made unenforceable against the debtor personally. Creditors whose claims against the debtor are discharged may never take action against the debtor to collect the discharged debts. If a creditor believes that the debtor should not receive a discharge under § 1141(d)(3)(C) of the Bankruptcy Code, timely action must be taken in the bankruptcy court in accordance with Bankruptcy Rule 4004(a). If a creditor believes that a debt owed to the creditor is not dischargeable under § 523(a)(2), (4), or (6) of the Bankruptcy Code, timely action must be taken in the bankruptcy court by the deadline set forth above in the box labeled "Discharge of Debts." Creditors considering taking such action may wish to seek legal advice.

PROOF OF CLAIM. Schedules of creditors have been or will be filed pursuant to Bankruptcy Rule 1007. Any creditor holding a scheduled claim which is not listed as disputed, contingent, or unliquidated as to amount may, but is not required to, file a proof of claim in this case. Creditors whose claims are not scheduled or whose claims are listed as disputed, contingent, or unliquidated as to amount and who desire to participate in the case or share in any distribution must file their proofs of claim. A creditor who desires to rely on the schedules of creditors has the responsibility for determining that the claim is listed accurately. If the court sets a deadline for filing a proof of claim, you will be notified. The place to file a proof of claim, either in person or by mail, is the office of the clerk of the bankruptcy court. Proof of claim forms are available in the clerk's office of any bankruptcy court.

PURPOSE OF CHAPTER 11 FILING. Chapter 11 of the Bankruptcy Code enables a debtor to reorganize pursuant to a plan. A plan is not effective unless approved by the court at a confirmation hearing. Creditors will be given notice concerning any plan, or in the event the case is dismissed or converted to another chapter of the Bankruptcy Code. The debtor will remain in possession of its property and will continue to operate any business unless a trustee is appointed.

Address of the Clerk of the Bankruptcy Court	For the Court:
	Clerk of the Bankruptcy Court
	Date

United States Bankruptcy Court

Case Number

______________ District of ______________

NOTICE OF COMMENCEMENT OF CASE UNDER CHAPTER 13 OF THE BANKRUPTCY CODE, MEETING OF CREDITORS, AND FIXING OF DATES

In re (Name of Debtor)	Address of Debtor	Soc. Sec. / Tax Id. Nos.
	Date Case Filed (or Converted)	
Name and Address of Attorney for Debtor	Name and Address of Trustee	
Telephone Number	Telephone Number	

☐ This is a converted case originally filed under chapter ______ on ______________________ (date).

FILING CLAIMS

Deadline to file a proof of Claim:

DATE, TIME, AND LOCATION OF MEETING OF CREDITORS

FILING OF PLAN AND DATE, TIME AND LOCATION OF HEARING ON CONFIRMATION OF PLAN

☐ The debtor has filed a plan. The plan or a summary of the plan is enclosed. Hearing on confirmation will be held:
______________(Date)______________(Time)________________________________(Location)

☐ The debtor has filed a plan. The plan or a summary of the plan and notice of the confirmation hearing will be sent separately.

☐ A plan has not been filed as of this date. Creditors will be given separate notice of the hearing on confirmation of the plan.

COMMENCEMENT OF CASE. An individual's debt adjustment case under chapter 13 of the Bankruptcy Code has been filed in this court by the debtor or debtors named above, and an order for relief has been entered. You will not receive notice of all documents filed in this case. All documents filed with the court, including lists of the debtor's property and debts, are available for inspection at the office of the clerk of the bankruptcy court.

CREDITORS MAY NOT TAKE CERTAIN ACTIONS. A creditor is anyone to whom the debtor owes money. Under the Bankruptcy Code, the debtor is granted certain protection against creditors. Common examples of prohibited actions by creditors are contacting the debtor to demand repayment, taking action against the debtor to collect money owed to creditors or to take property of the debtor, and starting or continuing foreclosure actions, repossessions, or wage deductions. Some protection is also given to certain codebtors of consumer debts. If unauthorized actions are taken by a creditor against a debtor, or a protected codebtor, the court may punish that creditor. A creditor who is considering taking action against the debtor or the property of the debtor, or any codebtor, should review §§ 362 and 1301 of the Bankruptcy Code and may wish to seek legal advice. The staff of the clerk of the bankruptcy court is not permitted to give legal advice.

MEETING OF CREDITORS. The debtor (both husband and wife in a joint case) is required to appear at the meeting of creditors on the date and at the place set forth above in the box labeled "Date, Time, and Location of Meeting of Creditors" for the purpose of being examined under oath. Attendance by creditors at the meeting is welcome, but not required. At the meeting, the creditors may examine the debtor and transact such other business as may properly come before the meeting. The meeting may be continued or adjourned from time to time by notice at the meeting, without further written notice to creditors.

PROOF OF CLAIM. Except as otherwise provided by law, in order to share in any payment from the estate, a creditor must file a proof of claim by the date set forth above in the box labeled "Filing Claims." The place to file the proof of claim, either in person or by mail, is the office of the clerk of the bankruptcy court. Proof of claim forms are available in the clerk's office of any bankruptcy court.

PURPOSE OF A CHAPTER 13 FILING. Chapter 13 of the Bankruptcy Code is designed to enable a debtor to pay debts in full or in part over a period of time pursuant to a plan. A plan is not effective unless approved by the bankruptcy court at a confirmation hearing. Creditors will be given notice in the event the case is dismissed or converted to another chapter of the Bankruptcy Code.

Address of the Clerk of the Bankruptcy Court	For the Court:
	Clerk of the Bankruptcy Court
	Date

UNITED STATES BANKRUPTCY COURT

_____________________ DISTRICT OF ___________________

In re ____,

[Set forth here all names including married, maiden, and trade names used by debtor within last 6 years.]

Debtor

Case No. ____________________

Chapter Seven

Social Security No(s). ____________________________ and all
Employer's Tax Identification Nos. *[If any]* ________________

____

DISCHARGE OF DEBTOR

It appearing that a petition commencing a case under title 11, United States Code, was filed by or against the person named above on ______________________, and that an order for relief was entered under chapter 7, and that no complaint objecting to the discharge of the debtor was filed within the time fixed by the court *[or* that a complaint objecting to discharge of the debtor was filed and, after due notice and hearing, was not sustained];

IT IS ORDERED that

1. The above - named debtor is released from all dischargeable debts.

2. Any judgment heretofore or hereafter obtained in any court other than this court is null and void as a determination of the personal liability of the debtor with respect to any of the following:

(a) debts dischargeable under 11 U.S.C. § 523;

(b) unless heretofore or hereafter determined by order of this court to be nondischargeable, debts alleged to be excepted from discharge under clauses (2), (4) and (6) of 11 U.S.C. § 523(a);

(c) debts determined by this court to be discharged.

3. All creditors whose debts are discharged by this order and all creditors whose judgments are declared null and void by paragraph 2 above are enjoined from instituting or continuing any action or employing any process or engaging in any act to collect such debts as personal liabilities of the above - named debtor.

Dated: ____________________________

BY THE COURT

____

United States Bankruptcy Judge.

Name______________________________________

Address____________________________________

____

Telephone _________________________________

☐ Attorney for Debtor(s) | (If applicable) Attorney's
☐ Debtor in Pro Se | State Bar I.D. No.______________

UNITED STATES BANKRUPTCY COURT
____________________ DISTRICT OF ____________________

In re ____________________________________,

[Set forth here all names including married, maiden, and trade names used by debtor within last 6 years.]

Debtor

Case No.____________________

Chapter 13

Social Security No(s) ____________________ and all
Employer's Tax Identification Nos.*[If any]*____________
____

DEBTOR'S PLAN AND MOTION TO AVOID LIENS

There shall be paid to the Chapter Thirteen Trustee $____________________ each month by debtors or any entity from whom debtors receive income, in such installments as agreed upon with the Trustee, for payment of all existing debts of debtors pursuant to this plan, except as the Court may otherwise order. Debtors submit all future income to the supervision and control of Trustee during the pendancy of this case and agree to pay sufficient funds to the Trustee to fully complete this plan.

1. ADMINISTRATIVE CLAIMS

Trustee shall disburse dividends to all §1322(a) claims and charges in advance of all other claims, unless their priority is expressly waived. All other §1322(a) and §1305(a)(1) claims allowed shall be paid in full by deferred payments in such priority and installments as the Trustee in his sole discretion deems appropriate.

2. UNSECURED CLAIMS

After dividends to other creditors pursuant to this plan, Trustee shall pay dividends prorata on claims allowed to %________ of the amount allowed in full satisfaction thereof. If left blank, pay 100%.

3. SECURED CLAIMS • PERSONAL PROPERTY

After payments provided for by paragraph one of this plan, Trustee shall make payment to creditors named in this paragraph whose claims are secured solely by personal property. Each named creditor shall be paid in installments from funds available for distribution monthly, noncumulative, as indicated until claim in amount filed and allowed plus interest at ten percent per annum is paid.

Name of Creditor	Fair Value	Installment
____________________	$____________	$____________
____________________	$____________	$____________
____________________	$____________	$____________
____________________	$____________	$____________
____________________	$____________	$____________
____________________	$____________	$____________

Holders of claims allowed as secured solely by personal property, other than those named above, shall be paid dividends prorata with such other creditors to the amount allowed secured creditors plus interest at ten percent per annum and in advance of distribution to general unsecured creditors.

Any creditor holding a lease on personal property in debtor's possession who files a claim herein and does not expressly reject this plan, shall be treated as a secured creditor, unless otherwise specifically treated.

In Re______________________ CaseNo.______________________

4. SECURED CREDITORS • REAL ESTATE

Except as otherwise provided, debtors during the pendency of this case shall make the usual and regular payments called for by any security agreements supporting nonvoidable liens against debtor's real estate directly to each lien holder in a current manner.

Arrearages to named lien holders shall be paid in installments by Trustee from funds available for distribution monthly, noncumulative, and, except for creditors specifically named in paragraph three above of this plan, shall be paid in advance of periodic distribution to other creditors. Payments shall be made in installments set forth below until amount allowed each lien holder on a claim for arrearages filed herein has been paid.

Lien Holder	Arrearages	Installments
______________________	$______________	$______________
______________________	$______________	$______________
______________________	$______________	$______________
______________________	$______________	$______________
______________________	$______________	$______________

Provisions of this paragraph shall operate to cure any default of any real estate security agreement notwithstanding that by terms of the security agreement or by the law or processes of a governmental unit the time for redemption or reinstatement has expired.

Notwithstanding any other provision of this paragraph, if debtors fail to make payment to the Trustee as provided by this plan, any funds held by Trustee may be distributed to creditors other than those provided for by this paragraph.

If there exist creditors not named in this paragraph holding statutory or other liens against debtors real estate and the obligation is fully due, for reasons other than exercise of a power of acceleration for failure to make installment payments, unless the Court under §362(d) orders otherwise, debtors will pay said claim directly to said creditor in full on or before six months following the date of confirmation of this plan.

5. CO-DEBTOR CLAIMS

Notwithstanding any other provision of this plan, creditors named in this paragraph who have allowed claims with a codebtor liable thereon, shall be paid 100% of the claim as allowed plus interest at the contract rate in installments as indicated by the Trustee. These installments are to be in advance of all claims except those allowed in paragraphs one, three and four from funds available for distribution monthly on a non-cumulative basis.

Name of Creditor	Installment
______________________	$______________
______________________	$______________
______________________	$______________

6. LIEN AVOIDANCE

Debtors hereby elect to avoid the fixing of liens pursuant to §522(b) of the Bankruptcy Code. All secured creditors, except those whose liens are avoidable pursuant to the provisions of §522(b) shall retain their liens until paid as provided for by this plan.

DEBTOR'S PLAN (Continued)

In Re________________________________ Case No.__________________________________

7. REJECTION OF CLAIM • SECURED CREDITOR

Debtors elect not to assume the lease or contract with creditors named in this paragraph and shall surrender to such creditor the collateral subject to the lien or lease in full satisfaction of any and all claims, secured or unsecured creditor may have against debtors arising from the transaction creating the interest of the creditor in the said property.

____

Name of Creditor

____

Name of Creditor

____

Name of Creditor

8. EXCLUSION OF CREDITOR

Notwithstanding any other provisions of this plan, debtors elect to assume the existing lease or contract with creditors named in this paragraph. These named creditors shall not be dealt with or provided for by this plan.

____

Name of Creditor

____

Name of Creditor

9. POST PETITION CLAIMS

Claims allowed for post petition debts incurred by debtors may be paid in full and in such order and on such terms as the Trustee, in his sole discretion, may determine. Trustee may file to dismiss this case if debtors incur post petition debts without the written consent of Trustee and debtors fail to keep such obligations current in payment.

10. GENERAL PROVISIONS

If this case is filed as a joint debtors case, the debtors' estates shall be fully consolidated for purposes of administration. Pursuant to §1322(b)(3) of the Bankruptcy Code, Trustee shall have the power to waive, in writing and on such conditions as the Trustee may impose, any default in debtors payments to Trustee under this plan.

11. OTHER PROVISIONS

Plan Dated ______________________

____

Debtor

____

Joint Debtor

BANKRUPTCY CODE SECTION 522(d)

1. The debtor's aggregate interest, not to exceed $15,000 in value, in real property or personal property that the debtor or a dependent of the debtor uses as a residence, in a cooperative that owns property that the debtor or a dependent of the debtor uses as a residence, or in a burial plot for the debtor or a dependent of the debtor.
2. The debtor's interest, not to exceed $2,400 in value, in one motor vehicle. A couple filing can each have a car with $2,400 equity.
3. The debtor's interest, not to exceed $400 in value in any particular item or $8,000 in aggregate value, in household furnishings, household goods, wearing apparel, appliances, books, animals, crops, or musical instruments, that are held primarily for the personal family or household use of the debtor or a dependent of the debtor.
4. The debtor's aggregate interest, not to exceed $1,000 in value, in jewelry held primarily for the personal, family, or household use of the debtor or a dependent of the debtor.
5. The debtor's aggregate interest in any property, not to exceed in value $800 plus up to $7,500 of any unused amount of the exemption provided under paragraph (1) of this subsection.
6. The debtor's aggregate interest, not to exceed $1,500 in value, in any implements, professional books, or tools of the trade of the debtor or the trade of a dependent of the debtor.
7. Any unmatured life insurance contract owned by the debtor, other than a credit life insurance contract.
8. The debtor's aggregate interest, not to exceed in value transferred in the manner specified in section 542(d) of this title, in any accrued dividend or interest under, or loan value of, any unmatured life insurance contract owned by the debtor under which the insured is the debtor or an individual of whom the debtor is a dependent.
9. Professionally prescribed health aids for the debtor or a dependent of the debtor.
10. The debtor's right to receive
    a. a Social Security benefit, unemployment compensation or a local public assistance benefit;
    b. a veteran's benefit;
    c. a disability, illness, or unemployment benefit;
    d. alimony, support, or separate maintenance, to the extent reasonably necessary for the support of the debtor and any dependent of the debtor;
    e. a payment under a stock bonus, pension, profit sharing, annuity, or similar plan or contract on account of illness, disability, death, age or length of service, to the extent reasonably necessary for the support of the debtor and any dependent of the debtor unless
        (i) such plan or contract was established by or under the auspices of an insider that employed the debtor at the time the debtor's rights under such plan or contract arose;
        (ii) such payment is on account of age or length of service; and
        (iii) such plan or contract does not qualify under the Internal Revenue Code.
11. The debtor's right to receive, or property that is traceable to
    a. an award under a crime victim's reparation law;
    b. a payment on account of the wrongful death of an individual of whom the debtor was a dependent, to the extent reasonably necessary for the support of the debtor and any dependent of the debtor;
    c. a payment under a life insurance contract that insured the life of an individual of whom the debtor was a dependent on the date of such individual's death, to the extent reasonably necessary for the support of the debtor and any dependent of the debtor;
    d. a payment, not to exceed $15,000, on account of personal bodily injury, not including pain and suffering or compensation for actual pecuniary loss, of the debtor or an individual of whom the debtor is a dependent; or
    e. a payment in compensation of loss of future earnings of the debtor or an individual of whom the debtor is or was a dependent, to the extent reasonably necessary for the support of the debtor and any dependent of the debtor.

WARNING: Laws and regulations are subject to change.
As a result, the accuracy of this exemption list is not guaranteed.
Check the laws of your state for any changes.

*All exemptions are 100% unless otherwise indicated.

ALABAMA

REAL ESTATE	Real property to $5,000; not in excess of 160 acres
PERSONAL PROPERTY/ HOUSEHOLD GOODS	Books; Burial place; Church pew; Clothing; Artwork/portraits
INSURANCE AND ANNUITIES	Annuity proceeds to $250 per month; Disability proceeds to $250 per month; Fraternal society benefits; Proceeds from life insurance if beneficiary is insured's spouse or child; Proceeds from life insurance if beneficiary is wife of insured; Life insurance proceeds if cannot be used to pay beneficiary's creditors
PENSIONS AND RETIREMENT PLANS	Law enforcement officers and judges; State employees; Teachers
PUBLIC BENEFITS AND ENTITLEMENTS	AFDC; Aid to blind, aged, disabled; Coal miners' benefits; Crime victims' compensation; Southeast Asian War POW's benefits; Unemployment compensation; Workers' compensation
WAGES	Bankruptcy: 75% of earned but unpaid wages.
MISCELLANEOUS	Business partnership property
WILD CARD	$3,000 of any personal property

In Bankruptcy you must claim the state not the federal exemptions.
(Alabama Code Title 6 Sec. 10-2; Sec. 10-5; Sec. 10-6; Sec. 10-7. Alabama Constitution Article X Sec. 204.)

ALASKA

REAL ESTATE	$54,000 in property
PERSONAL PROPERTY/ HOUSEHOLD GOODS	Motor vehicle to $3,000; Books, musical instruments, clothing, household goods & heirlooms to $3,000; Building materials; Burial place; Pets to $1,000; Proceeds for damaged exempt property; Wrongful death recoveries; Recovery for personal injury
INSURANCE AND ANNUITIES	Disability benefits; Benefits from fraternal society; Insurance proceeds for personal injury or wrongful death; Life insurance or annuity; Accrued dividends and loan value to $10,000; Life insurance proceeds if beneficiary is insured's spouse or dependent; Medical benefits
PENSIONS AND RETIREMENT PLANS	ERISA; Public employees; Teachers; Other pensions
PUBLIC BENEFITS AND ENTITLEMENTS	Unemployment compensation; Workers' compensation; AFDC; Adult assistance to elderly, blind, disabled; Alaska longevity bonus; Crime victims' compensation; Federally exempt public benefits paid or due; General relief assistance; 50% of permanent fund dividends
WAGES	Weekly net earnings to $350; Sole wage earner in household $2,200
MISCELLANEOUS	Alimony and child support; Liquor licenses; Business partnership property; Books & tools of trade to $2,800

In Bankruptcy you must claim the state not the federal exemptions.
(Alaska Statues Sec. 9.38.010; Sec. 9.38. 017; Sec. 9.38.025; Sec. 9.30.020; Sec. 9.30.15; Sec. 9.38.030.)

ARIZONA

REAL ESTATE	Real estate to $100,000 (total exemption claimed by both spouses). Sale proceeds exempt 18 months after sale or until new home purchased, whichever occurs first
PERSONAL PROPERTY/ HOUSEHOLD GOODS	Bible; bicycle; sewing machine; typewriter; burial plot to $500 total; Books to $250; Clothing to $500; Furniture and furnishings to $4,000; Wedding & engagement rings to $1,000; Watch to $100; Pets, horses, milk cows & poultry to $500; Musical instruments to $250; Prostheses, including wheelchair; Motor vehicle to $1,500-$4,000 if disabled; Prepaid rent or security deposit to $1,000 or 1 1/2 months' rent, whichever is less; Bank deposit to $150 in one account; Proceeds for sold or damaged exempt property; Food, fuel and provisions for 6 months.
INSURANCE AND ANNUITIES	Group life insurance policy or proceeds; Health accident or disability benefits; Life insurance cash value to $25,000 if beneficiary is dependent; Life insurance proceeds to $20,000 if beneficiary is spouse or child; Fraternal society benefits
PENSIONS AND RETIREMENT PLANS	Board of regents members; Elected officials; ERISA; Firefighters and police officers; State employees
PUBLIC BENEFITS AND ENTITLEMENTS	Unemployment compensation; Workers' Compensation; Welfare benefits
WAGES	Bankruptcy: Minimum 75% of earned but unpaid wages, pension payments.
MISCELLANEOUS	Minor child's earnings; Business partnership property; Farm machinery, utensils, feed, & animals to $1,500; Teacher aids; Equipment, instruments & books to $2,500

In Bankruptcy you must claim the state not the federal exemptions.
(Arizona Revised Statutes Sec. 33-1101; Sec. 33-1123; Sec. 33-1124; Sec. 33-1125; Sec. 33-1126; Sec. 33-1130; Sec. 33-1131.)

ARKANSAS

REAL ESTATE	Choose one or the other, not both: 1. Rural homestead of 80-160 acres to $2,500; urban homestead of 1/4 to 1 acre to $2,500 2. Real or personal property used as residence to $800 if single; $1,250 if married
PERSONAL PROPERTY/ HOUSEHOLD GOODS	Burial plot to 5 acres, in lieu of homestead option 2; Clothing; Motor vehicle to $1,200; Wedding rings with diamonds not exceeding 1/2 carat
INSURANCE AND ANNUITIES	Disability benefits; Group life insurance; Life, health, accident or disability proceeds, Annuity contract; Fraternal society benefits; Mutual assessment insurance benefits to $1,000.
PENSIONS AND RETIREMENT PLANS	Disabled firefighters and police officers; Firefighters and police officers; IRA deposits to $20,000 (limit applies to individual debtor and husband/wife combined), if deposits exceed 1 year before attachment by creditor or bankruptcy; School employees
PUBLIC BENEFITS AND ENTITLEMENTS	Public assistance; Crime victims' compensation; Unemployment compensation; Workers' compensation

WAGES	Earned but unpaid wages due for 60 days but not under $25 per week
MISCELLANEOUS	Business partnership property; Tools of trade to $750
WILD CARD	$500 of any personal property if married or head of family; individuals $200

In Bankruptcy you may claim the state exemptions or the federal exemptions.
(Arkansas Statutes Sec. 30-207; Sec. 36-211. Arkansas Constitution Article 9 Sec. 3-5; Sec. 1, 2.)

CALIFORNIA - SYSTEM 1

REAL ESTATE	Real property, mobile home, co-op, or condo to $50,000 if single & not disabled; $75,000 for families; $100,000 if 65 or older or disabled; $100,000 if 55 or older, single & earn under $15,000 or married & earn under $20,000. Sale proceeds exempt for 6 months after received.
PERSONAL PROPERTY/ HOUSEHOLD GOODS	Furnishings, clothing & food; Burial place; Bank deposits from Social Security to $500; $750 if 2 or more payees; Building materials to $1,000; Jewelry, heirlooms & art to $2,500 total; Motor vehicles to $1,200; Personal injury claims or recoveries; Wrongful death causes of action or recoveries; Proceeds from exempt property
INSURANCE AND ANNUITIES	Disability or health benefits; Fidelity bonds; Fraternal benefits: Life insurance to $4,000, Unemployment benefits; Life insurance; Unmatured life insurance policy to $4,000 loan value
PENSIONS AND RETIREMENT PLANS	Private retirement benefits, IRAs & Keoghs; Public employees; Public retirement benefits
PUBLIC BENEFITS AND ENTITLEMENTS	Union benefits due to labor dispute; Workers' compensation; Aid to blind, aged, disabled; AFDC; Financial aid to students; Relocation benefits; Unemployment benefits
WAGES	Public employees vacation credits; 75% unless earning are subject to support orders or assignments.
MISCELLANEOUS	Business or professional licenses, except liquor license; Inmates' trust funds to $1,000; Business partnership property; County employees; Tools, materials, uniforms, books, furnishings, equipment, motor vehicle to $2,500 total; to $5,000 total if both spouses use in same occupation. Motor vehicle cannot be claimed under tools of trade exemption if claimed under personal property.

In Bankruptcy you may choose state exemptions in System 1 or System 2, but not federal exemptions.
(California Code of Civil Procedure Sec. 703.080; Sec. 703.130; Sec. 704.010; Sec. 704.020; Sec. 704.030; Sec. 704.040; Sec. 704.050; Sec. 704.060; Sec. 704.070; Sec. 704.080; Sec. 704.090; Sec. 704.113; Sec. 704.140; Sec. 704.150; Sec. 704.200; Sec. 704.730; Sec. 704.050.)

CALIFORNIA - SYSTEM 2

REAL ESTATE	Real property and co-ops to $7,500; unused homestead may be applied to other property
PERSONAL PROPERTY/ HOUSEHOLD GOODS	Animals, crops, appliances, furnishings, household goods, books, musical instruments & clothing to $200 per item; Burial plot to $7,500, if homestead is not claimed; Jewelry to $500 total; Motor vehicle to $1,200; Personal injury recoveries to $7,500; Wrongful death recoveries
INSURANCE AND ANNUITIES	Disability benefits; Fidelity bonds; Life insurance proceeds; Unmatured life insurance policy with dividends or loan value to $4,000
PENSIONS AND RETIREMENT PLANS	ERISA

PUBLIC BENEFITS AND ENTITLEMENTS	Unemployment compensation; Veterans' benefits; Crime victims' compensation; Public assistance; Social security
MISCELLANEOUS	Business partnership property; Alimony, child support; Business or professional licenses, except liquor license; Tools of trade to $750; prescribed health aids
WILD CARD	$400 of any property; Unused portion of homestead or burial exemption, of any property

In Bankruptcy you may choose state exemptions in System 1 or System 2, but not federal exemptions.
(California Code of Civil Procedure Sec. 703.140.)

COLORADO

REAL ESTATE	Real property or mobile home up to $30,000
PERSONAL PROPERTY/ HOUSEHOLD GOODS	Pictures & Books to $750; Burial place; Clothing to $750; Food & fuel to $300; Household goods to $1,500; Jewelry to $500 total; Motor vehicles if used in occupation to $1,000 or if owned by disabled or elderly person and used to obtain medical care, to $3,000; Personal injury recoveries, unless debt related to injury; Proceeds for damaged exempt property
INSURANCE AND ANNUITIES	Disability benefits to $200 per month; lump sum exempt; Fraternal society benefits; Group life insurance; Homeowners' insurance (same as homestead exemption); Life insurance to $5,000; Life insurance if cannot be used to pay beneficiary's creditors
PENSIONS AND RETIREMENT PLANS	ERISA; Firefighters and police; Public employees; Teachers
PUBLIC BENEFITS AND ENTITLEMENTS	Veteran's benefits; Workers' compensation; AFDC; Aid to blind, aged, disabled; Crime victims' compensation;Unemployment compensation
WAGES	Bankruptcy: Minimum 75% of earned but unpaid wages, pension payments
MISCELLANEOUS	Business partnership property; Horses, machinery, harness & tools of farmer to $2,000 total; Library of professional to $1,500 or stock in trade, supplies, fixtures, machines, tools, equipment & books to $1,500 total; Livestock of farmer to $3,000

In Bankruptcy you must claim the state not the federal exemptions.
(Colorado Revised Statutes Sec. 13-54-102; Sec. 13-54-104; Sec. 38-41-201; Sec. 38-41-201.6.)

CONNECTICUT

REAL ESTATE	Real property to $75,000; insurance proceeds on exempt property
PERSONAL PROPERTY/ HOUSEHOLD GOODS	Utility and security deposits for residence; Appliances & furniture; Motor vehicle to $1,500; Wedding & engagement rings; Clothing, food and bedding; Burial place
INSURANCE AND ANNUITIES	Benefits paid under no-fault insurance law; Disability benefits paid by association for its members; Fraternal benefit society benefits; Health and disability benefits; Life insurance proceeds if cannot be used to pay beneficiary's creditors; Unmatured life insurance to $4,000
PENSIONS AND RETIREMENT PLANS	ERISA; State employees; Teachers

PUBLIC BENEFITS	Veterans' benefits; Workers' compensation; Public assistance benefits; Crime victims' compensation; Social security; Unemployment compensation
WAGES	Bankruptcy: Minimum 75% of earned but unpaid wages; Judgment creditor: Greater of 75% of your weekly net earnings or $114 per week
MISCELLANEOUS	Alimony and child support; Business partnership property; Tools, books, instruments, farm animals, feed and property necessary to a farming operation; Prescribed health aids; Military equipment owned by members of the armed services
WILD CARD	Any property to $1,000

In Bankruptcy, you may claim either the state or the federal exemptions.
(Connecticut General Statutes Annotated Sec. 52-352b; Sec. 83-581.)

DELAWARE

REAL ESTATE	Property to $5,000 per debtor; Property held as tenancy by the entirety exempt against debt of only one spouse
PERSONAL PROPERTY/ HOUSEHOLD GOODS	Clothing and jewelry; Burial place; Church pew; Pianos, organs & sewing machines; School books, family Bible, family pictures & family library
INSURANCE AND ANNUITIES	Annuity contract proceeds to $350 per month; Employee life insurance; Health or disability benefits; Life insurance proceeds if cannot be used to pay beneficiary's creditors; Fraternal society benefits
PENSIONS AND RETIREMENT PLANS	Kent County employees; Police officers & Volunteer firefighters; State employees
PUBLIC BENEFITS AND ENTITLEMENTS	Unemployment compensation; Workers' compensation; Aid to blind; Aid to aged, disabled; AFDC; General assistance
WAGES	85% of earned but unpaid wages
MISCELLANEOUS	Business partnership property; Tools, implements & fixtures to $75 in New Castle & Sussex Counties; to $50 in Kent County
WILD CARD	$500 of any personal property, if head of family

In Bankruptcy you must claim the state not the federal exemptions.
(Delaware Code Annotated Title Sec. 4902; Sec. 4903; Sec. 4913.)

DISTRICT OF COLUMBIA

REAL ESTATE	None. Exception, property held as tenancy by the entirety exempt against debt of only one spouse
PERSONAL PROPERTY/ HOUSEHOLD GOODS	Cooking utensils, stoves, furniture, furnishings, radios & sewing machines to $300; Books to $400; Clothing to $300; Cooperative association holdings to $50; Residential condominium deposit; Food and fuel for 3 months
INSURANCE AND ANNUITIES	Fraternal benefit society benefits; Disability benefits; Life insurance proceeds cannot be used to pay creditors; Group life insurance; Life insurance proceeds; Other insurance proceeds to $200 per month, maximum 2 months, for head of family; else $60 per month
PENSIONS AND RETIREMENT PLANS	Public school teachers

PUBLIC BENEFITS AND ENTITLEMENTS	Unemployment compensation; Workers' compensation; Aid to blind, aged, disabled; AFDC; Crime victims' compensation; General assistance
WAGES	Bankruptcy: Minimum 75% of earned but unpaid wages, pension payments; Judgment creditor: Greater of 75% of your weekly net earnings or $114 per week; Non-wage and non-pension earnings for 60 days to $200 per month for head of family; else $60 per month
MISCELLANEOUS	Business partnership property; Library, furniture, tools of professional or artist to $300; Mechanic's tools; tools of trade or business to $200; Motor vehicle, cart, wagon & horse to $500; Stock & materials to $200

In Bankruptcy you may claim either the state or the federal exemptions.
(District of Columbia Code Sec. 15-501; Sec. 15-503; Sec. 35-521 through 35-525.)

FLORIDA

REAL ESTATE	Real property including mobile home to unlimited value; property cannot exceed 1/2 acre in municipality or 160 contiguous acres elsewhere; Tenancy by the entirety property exempt against debt of only one spouse
PERSONAL PROPERTY/ HOUSEHOLD GOODS	Personal property to $1,000; Automobile up to $1,000
INSURANCE AND ANNUITIES	Annuity contract proceeds; Death benefits payable to a specific beneficiary, not the deceased's estate; Disability or illness benefits; Fraternal society benefits; Cash surrender value of life insurance
PENSIONS AND RETIREMENT PLANS	County officers, employees; ERISA; Police officers and firefighters; State officers, employees; Teachers
PUBLIC BENEFITS AND ENTITLEMENTS	Veterans' benefits; Workers' compensation; Crime victims' compensation; Public assistance; Social security; Unemployment compensation
WAGES	$500 per week for head of family; Greater of 75% or 30 times minimum wage per week for others; 3 months of federal government pension if needed to support debtor or family.
MISCELLANEOUS	Alimony, child support; Business partnership property; Prescribed health aids
WILD CARD	See personal property

In Bankruptcy you must claim the state not the federal exemptions.
(Florida Statutes Annotated Sec. 222.05; Sec. 222-11. Florida Constitution Article 10 Sec. 4.)

GEORGIA

REAL ESTATE	Real property, including co-op to $5,000; unused homestead may be applied to any property
PERSONAL PROPERTY/ HOUSEHOLD GOODS	Burial place; Jewelry to $500; Motor vehicles to $1,000; Personal injury recoveries to $7,500; Wrongful death recoveries; Animals, crops, clothing, books, household goods, musical instruments to $200 per item, $3,500 maximum
INSURANCE AND ANNUITIES	Annuity & endowment benefits; Disability or health benefits to $250 per month; Fraternal society benefits; Life insurance proceeds if needed for support; Life insurance proceeds if beneficiary not the insured; Unmatured life insurance dividends, interest, loan value or cash value to $2,000

PENSIONS AND RETIREMENT PLANS	ERISA; Public employees; Any pension needed for support
PUBLIC BENEFITS AND ENTITLEMENTS	Veterans' benefits; Workers' compensation; Aid to blind and disabled; Crime victims' compensation; Local public assistance; Social security; Old age assistance; Unemployment compensation;
WAGES	Bankruptcy: Minimum 75% of earned but unpaid wages for private & federal workers; Judgment creditor: Greater of 75% of your weekly net earnings or $114 per week
MISCELLANEOUS	Alimony, child support; Books & tools of trade to $500
WILD CARD	$400 of any property; Unused portion of homestead exemption

In Bankruptcy you must claim the state not the federal exemptions.
(Georgia Code Annotated Sec. 44-13-100.)

HAWAII

REAL ESTATE	Head of family or over 65 to $30,000; Others to $20,00.
PERSONAL PROPERTY/ HOUSEHOLD GOODS	Burial place; Clothing; Jewelry to $1,000; Motor vehicle to $1,000 (wholesale value); Furnishings, appliances & books
INSURANCE AND ANNUITIES	Annuity or endowment policy; Disability benefits; Fraternal society benefits; Group life insurance; Life or health insurance policy for spouse or child
PENSIONS AND RETIREMENT PLANS	ERISA; Police officers & firefighters; Public officers & employees
PUBLIC BENEFITS AND ENTITLEMENTS	Workers' compensation; Unemployment compensation; Unemployment work relief funds to $60 per month; Public assistance paid by DSSH
WAGES	Unpaid wages due for services of past 31 days; after 31 days, 95% of 1st $100; 90% of 2nd $100; 80% of balance; Prisoner's wages held by DSSH
MISCELLANEOUS	Business partnership property; Tools, implements, books, instruments, uniforms, furnishings, motor vehicle & other personal property needed for livelihood

In Bankruptcy you may claim either the state or the federal exemptions.
(Hawaii Revised Statutes Sec. 651-92; Sec. 651-121.)

IDAHO

REAL ESTATE	$50,000; proceeds from sale exempt for 6 months
PERSONAL PROPERTY/ HOUSEHOLD GOODS	Books, furnishings, appliances, clothing, pets, musical instruments, 1 firearm, family portraits & heirlooms to $500 per item, $4,000 total; Building materials; Burial place; Jewelry to $250; Motor vehicle to $1,500; Personal injury recoveries needed for support; Wrongful death recoveries; Crops to $1,000 with water rights to 160 inches; Equipment necessary to perform military or police work
INSURANCE AND ANNUITIES	Annuity contract proceeds to $350 per month; Death or disability benefits; Fraternal society benefits; Homeowners' insurance proceeds to $25,000; Life insurance; Medical benefits
PENSIONS AND RETIREMENT PLANS	ERISA; Firefighters and police officers; Public employees; Any pensions needed for support

PUBLIC BENEFITS AND ENTITLEMENTS	Veterans' benefits; Workers' compensation; Aid to blind, aged, disabled; AFDC; Crime victims' compensation unless debt for treatment of injury incurred during the crime; Any type of government assistance; General assistance; Social Security; Unemployment compensation;
WAGES	Bankruptcy: Minimum 75% of earned but unpaid wages, pension payments; Judgment creditor: Greater of 75% of your weekly net earnings or $114 per week
MISCELLANEOUS	Alimony, child support needed for support; Liquor licenses; Business partnership property; Books & tools of trade to $1,000

In Bankruptcy you must claim the state not the federal exemptions.
(Idaho Code Sec. 11-207; Sec. 11-603; Sec. 11-604; Sec. 11-605; Sec. 55-1003.)

ILLINOIS

REAL ESTATE	Real property to $7,500; Proceeds from sale exempt 1 year from date of sale
PERSONAL PROPERTY/ HOUSEHOLD GOODS	Family pictures, school books, clothing; Vehicles to $1,200; personal injury recoveries to $7,500; exempt property proceeds; wrongful death recoveries needed for support
INSURANCE AND ANNUITIES	Health or disability benefits; Homeowners' proceeds for destroyed home, to $7,500; Life insurance, annuity proceeds or cash value if beneficiary is insured's child, parent, spouse or other dependent; Fraternal society benefits;Life insurance proceeds if cannot be used to pay beneficiary's creditors; Life insurance proceeds needed for support
PENSIONS AND RETIREMENT PLANS	Civil service employees; county employees; Disabled firefighters; widows & children of firefighters; ERISA; General assembly members; Municipal employees; Police officers and firefighters; State university employees; Teachers
PUBLIC BENEFITS AND ENTITLEMENTS	Veterans' benefits; Workers' compensation; Aid to aged, blind, disabled; AFDC; Crime victims' compensation; Social Security; Unemployment compensation
WAGES	Bankruptcy: Minimum 85% of earned but unpaid wages; Judgment creditor: Greater of 75% of your weekly net earnings or $114 per week
MISCELLANEOUS	Alimony, child support; Business partnership property; Implements, books & tools of trade to $750
WILD CARD	$2,000 of any personal property

In Bankruptcy you must claim the state not the federal exemptions.
(Illinois Code of Civil Procedure Sec. 12-8903; Sec. 12-901; Sec. 12-1001.)

INDIANA

REAL ESTATE	Real property claimed as residence to $7,500. In addition, homestead plus personal property (except health aids) up to $10,000. Also, property held as tenancy by the entirety is exempt against debt of only one spouse
PERSONAL PROPERTY/ HOUSEHOLD GOODS	$4,000 of tangible personal property; $100, any intangible personal property; except funds due
INSURANCE AND ANNUITIES	Fraternal society benefits; Life insurance; Accident proceeds
PENSIONS AND RETIREMENT PLANS	Firefighters, police, sheriffs; Public employees; State teachers

PUBLIC BENEFITS AND ENTITLEMENTS	Unemployment compensation; Workers' compensation; Crime victims' compensation unless debt for treatment of injury incurred during the crime
WAGES	Bankruptcy: Minimum 75% of earned but unpaid wages; Judgment creditor: Greater of 75% of your weekly net earnings or $114 per week
MISCELLANEOUS	Business partnership property; State military personnel's uniforms, arms & equipment
WILD CARD	See personal property

In Bankruptcy you must claim the state not the federal exemptions.
(Indiana Statutes Annotated Sec. 24-4.5-5-105; Sec. 34-2-28-1.)

IOWA

REAL ESTATE	Real property unlimited value; property cannot exceed 1/2 acre in town or city, 40 acres elsewhere
PERSONAL PROPERTY/ HOUSEHOLD GOODS	Furnishings & household goods to $2,000; Books, pictures & paintings to $1,000; Burial plot to 1 acre; Clothing to $1,000; Motor vehicle & musical instruments to $5,000; Wedding or engagement rings (received prior to marriage).
INSURANCE AND ANNUITIES	Accident, disability, health, illness or life proceeds to $15,000; Employee group insurance; Benefits from fraternal benefit society; Life insurance proceeds to $10,000 for first two years of policy paid to spouse, child or other dependent
PENSIONS AND RETIREMENT PLANS	Firefighters, police; public employees; Other pensions needed for support
PUBLIC BENEFITS AND ENTITLEMENTS	Veterans' benefits; Workers' compensation; Adopted child assistance; AFDC; Social Security; Unemployment compensation
WAGES	Bankruptcy: Minimum 75% of earned but unpaid wages, pension payments
MISCELLANEOUS	Alimony, child support needed for support; Liquor licenses; Business partnership property; Farming equipment, including livestock, feed to $10,000; Non-farming equipment to $10,000
WILD CARD	$100 of any personal property

In Bankruptcy you must claim the state not the federal exemptions.
(Iowa Code Annotated Sec. 561.2; Sec. 627.6; Sec. 642.21.)

KANSAS

REAL ESTATE	Real property & mobile home under 1 acre in town or city, 160 acres rural
PERSONAL PROPERTY/ HOUSEHOLD GOODS	Burial place; Funeral plan prepayments; Clothing; Food & fuel; Furnishings & household equipment; Jewelry to $1,000; Motor vehicle to $20,000
INSURANCE AND ANNUITIES	Life insurance
PENSIONS AND RETIREMENT PLANS	Officials in cities with populations between 120,000 & 200,000; ERISA; Police officers & firefighters; Government employees; State school employees
PUBLIC BENEFITS AND ENTITLEMENTS	Unemployment compensation; Workers' compensation; AFDC; Crime victims' compensation; Social welfare; General assistance

WAGES	Bankruptcy: Minimum 75% of earned but unpaid wages; Judgment creditor: Greater of 75% of your weekly net earnings or $114 per week
MISCELLANEOUS	Liquor licenses; Business partnership property; Books, documents, furniture, instruments, equipment, to $7,500 total

In Bankruptcy you must claim the state not the federal exemptions.
(Kansas Statutes Annotated Sec. 60-2301; Sec. 60-2304.)

KENTUCKY

REAL ESTATE	Real or personal property claimed as residence to $5,000
PERSONAL PROPERTY/ HOUSEHOLD GOODS	Burial plot to $5,000; Clothing, jewelry, & furnishings to $3,000 total; Payments for lost earnings needed for support; Medical expenses; Reparation benefits; Motor vehicle to $2,500; Personal injury recoveries to $7,500 (not to include pain & suffering); Wrongful death recoveries
INSURANCE AND ANNUITIES	Health or disability or annuity contract benefits; Cooperative life or casualty insurance benefits; Life insurance policy of spouse beneficiary; Fraternal society benefits; Life insurance proceeds if proceeds cannot be used to pay beneficiary's creditors
PENSIONS AND RETIREMENT PLANS	Firefighters, police, teachers; State employees; County government employees; Other pensions needed for support, IRAs
PUBLIC BENEFITS AND ENTITLEMENTS	Unemployment compensation; Workers' compensation; Aid to blind, aged, disabled, AFDC; Crime victims' compensation
WAGES	Bankruptcy: Minimum 75% of earned but unpaid wages.
MISCELLANEOUS	Alimony, child support; Business partnership property; Furnishings of minister, attorney, physician, veterinarian or dentist to $1,000; Motor vehicle of mechanic, minister, attorney, physician, veterinarian or dentist to $2,500; Tools, equipment, livestock of farmer to $3,000; Tools of non-farmer to $300
WILD CARD	$1,000 of any property

In Bankruptcy you must claim the state not the federal exemptions.
(Kentucky Revised Statutes Sec. 427.010; Sec. 427.030; Sec. 427.040; Sec. 427.060; Sec. 427.150; Sec. 427.160.)

LOUISIANA

REAL ESTATE	$15,000; property cannot exceed 160 acres
PERSONAL PROPERTY/ HOUSEHOLD GOODS	Furniture, utensils, clothing, family portraits, musical instruments, heating & cooling equipment; pressing irons, sewing machine, refrigerator, freezer, stove, washer & dryer; Burial place; Engagement & wedding rings to $5,000
INSURANCE AND ANNUITIES	Fraternal society benefits; Insurance policies or proceeds; Health, accident or disability proceeds
PENSIONS AND RETIREMENT PLANS	ERISA
PUBLIC BENEFITS AND ENTITLEMENTS	Unemployment compensation; Workers' compensation; Aid to blind, aged, disabled, AFDC; Crime victims' compensation
WAGES	Bankruptcy: Minimum 75% of earned but unpaid wages; Judgment creditor: Greater of 75% of your weekly net earnings or $114 per week

MISCELLANEOUS	Minor child's property; Tools, instruments, books, truck (maximum 3 tons) or non-luxury auto & utility trailer

In Bankruptcy you must claim the state not the federal exemptions.
(Louisiana Revised Statutes Sec. 13:3881; Sec. 20:1.)

MAINE

REAL ESTATE	Real, co-op or burial plot to $12,500; if living with minors to $25,000; if debtor over 60 or physically or mentally disabled, to $60,000. Unused residence exemption to $6,000
PERSONAL PROPERTY/ HOUSEHOLD GOODS	Animals crops, musical instruments, books, clothing, furnishings, household goods to $200 per item. Furnaces, stoves and fuel; Jewelry to $750; Payments for lost earnings needed for support; Motor vehicle to $2,500; Personal injury and wrongful death recoveries to $12,500 (not pain & suffering); Prescribed health aids; Food and produce for 6 months
INSURANCE AND ANNUITIES	Life insurance policy; Life insurance payments to debtor necessary for support; Disability benefits and pensions; Group health or life policy or proceeds; Fraternal society benefits
PENSIONS AND RETIREMENT PLANS	ERISA; Legislators; State employees
PUBLIC BENEFITS AND ENTITLEMENTS	Veterans' benefits; Workers' compensation; AFDC; Crime victims' compensation; Social Security; Unemployment compensation
WAGES	Greater of 75% or 30 times the minimum hourly wage per week.
MISCELLANEOUS	Alimony & child support; Business partnership property; Commercial fishing boat to 5 tons; Materials & stock to $1,000; 1 of each type of farm implement; Fertilizer, feed, seed, etc. for 1 growing season; Tools of the trade to $5,000
WILD CARD	$400 of any property

In Bankruptcy you must claim the state not the federal exemptions.
(Maine Revised Statutes Annotated Title 14 Sec. 4422.)

MARYLAND

REAL ESTATE	None. Tenancy by the entirety property exempt against debt of one spouse
PERSONAL PROPERTY/ HOUSEHOLD GOODS	Appliances, furnishings, household goods, books, pets & clothing to $500 total; Burial place; Cash or any property up to $3,000; Recovery for lost future earnings
INSURANCE AND ANNUITIES	Medical benefits deducted from wages; Disability or health benefits; Fraternal society benefits; Life insurance
PENSIONS AND RETIREMENT PLANS	ERISA (except IRAs); Deceased Baltimore police officers; State employees; Teachers
PUBLIC BENEFITS AND ENTITLEMENTS	Unemployment compensation; Workers' compensation; AFDC; Crime victims' compensation; General assistance
WAGES	Earned but unpaid wages; Greater of 75% or $145 per week in Kent, Caroline, & Queen Anne's of Worcester Counties; Greater of 75% of actual wages or $114 per week
MISCELLANEOUS	Business partnership property; Clothing, books, tools, instruments & appliances to $2,500

WILD CARD	$2,500 of any property, real or personal

In Bankruptcy you must claim the state not the federal exemptions.
(Maryland Annotated Code of Commercial Law Sec. 15-601.1; Maryland Annotated Code of Cts. and Jud. Proc. Sec. 11-504.)

MASSACHUSETTS

REAL ESTATE	$100,000; Tenancy by the entirety property exempt against debt of only one spouse.
PERSONAL PROPERTY/ HOUSEHOLD GOODS	Bank deposits to $125; Clothing; Books to $200 total; sewing machine to $200; Cash for fuel, heat, water or light to $75 per month; Cash to $200 per month for rent; Co-op shares to $100; Furniture to $3,000; Motor vehicle to $700; Trust company, bank deposits to $500; Burial places, & church pew
INSURANCE AND ANNUITIES	Benefits from fraternal benefit society; Life or endowment policy, proceeds or cash value; Group annuity policy or proceeds; Life insurance policy if beneficiary is married woman or cannot be used to pay beneficiary's creditors; Disability benefits to $35 per week; Group life insurance policy
PENSIONS AND RETIREMENT PLANS	Private retirement benefits; Public employees; Savings bank employees
PUBLIC BENEFITS AND ENTITLEMENTS	Veterans' benefits, Workers' compensation; AFDC, Aid to aged, Disabled, Unemployment compensation
WAGES	Earned but unpaid wages to $125 per week; Payment (wage or pension) being received to $100 per week
MISCELLANEOUS	Business partnership property; Boats, fishing tackle of fisherman to $500; Tools, & fixtures to $500 total

In Bankruptcy you may claim either the state or the federal exemptions.
(Massachusetts General Laws Annotated Chap. 188 Sec. 1; Chap. 235 Sec. 34; Chap. 246 Sec. 28A; Chap. 175.)

MICHIGAN

REAL ESTATE	Real estate to $3,500; property cannot exceed 1 lot, or 40 acres rural. In addition, tenancy by the entirety property exempt against debt of only one spouse
PERSONAL PROPERTY/ HOUSEHOLD GOODS	Building & loan association shares to $1,000 par value, in lieu of homestead; Burial place; Church pew, clothing; family pictures; Appliances, books, household goods to $1,000 total; Food & fuel for 6 months
INSURANCE AND ANNUITIES	Life, endowment or annuity proceeds if cannot be used to pay beneficiary's creditors; Life or endowment proceeds if beneficiary is insured's spouse or child; Life insurance proceeds if beneficiary is married; Benefits from fraternal benefit society; Disability, mutual life or health benefits
PENSIONS AND RETIREMENT PLANS	Firefighters, police officers; IRAs except contributions made within 120 days of filing; Legislators, Public school employees, State employees
PUBLIC BENEFITS AND ENTITLEMENTS	Veterans' benefits for veterans; Workers' compensation; AFDC; Crime victims' compensation; Social welfare benefits; Unemployment compensation
WAGES	60% of earned but unpaid wages for head of household; else 40%
MISCELLANEOUS	Business partnership property; Tools, implements, materials, stock, motor vehicle, horse & harness to $1,000 total

In Bankruptcy you may claim either the state or the federal exemptions.
(Michigan Compiled Laws Annotated Sec. 600.6023.)

MINNESOTA

REAL ESTATE	Real property to $200,000 generally, $500,000 if used in farming, cannot exceed 1/2 acre in city or 160 acres rural
PERSONAL PROPERTY/ HOUSEHOLD GOODS	Burial place; Church pew; motor vehicle to $2,000 ($20,000 if modified for disabled person); Appliances, furniture, radio, phonographs & TV to $4,500 total; Clothing, food & utensils; Personal injury and wrongful death recoveries; Proceeds for damaged exempt property; Books & musical instruments
INSURANCE AND ANNUITIES	Accident or disability proceeds; Life insurance or endowment proceeds if beneficiary isn't the insured; Life insurance proceeds if beneficiary is spouse or child of insured to $20,000, plus $5,000 per dependent; Police, fire benefits; Unmatured life insurance contract dividends, interest or loan value to $4,000; Fraternal society benefits
PENSIONS AND	ERISA, including IRAs; Private retirement benefits; Public employees and state employees
PUBLIC BENEFITS AND ENTITLEMENTS	Veterans' benefits; Workman compensation; AFDC; General or supplemental assistance; Supplemental security income; Crime victims' compensation; Unemployment compensation
WAGES	Bankruptcy: Minimum 75% of earned but unpaid wages; Wages deposited into bank accounts for 20 days after depositing; Wages of released inmates paid within 6 months of release
MISCELLANEOUS	Minor child's earnings; Business partnership property; Farm machines, livestock, crops of farmers to $13,000 total; School teacher materials; Tools, machines, instruments, furniture, stock in trade & library to $5,000 total

In Bankruptcy you may claim either the state or the federal exemptions.
(Minnesota Statutes Annotated Sec. 550.37.)

MISSISSIPPI

REAL ESTATE	$75,000; property cannot exceed 160 acres
PERSONAL PROPERTY/ HOUSEHOLD GOODS	Personal injury judgments to $10,000;Tangible personal property to $10,000
INSURANCE AND ANNUITIES	Disability benefits; Homeowners' insurance to $75,000 if exempt homestead; Life insurance to $50,000; Fraternal society benefits; Life insurance proceeds payable to another to $50,000; Life insurance proceeds payable to insured's estate to $5,000.
PENSIONS AND RETIREMENT PLANS	ERISA benefits deposited over 1 year before creditor attachment or filing for bankruptcy; IRAs and Keoghs; Private retirement benefits; Police officers, firefighters; State employees; Teachers
PUBLIC BENEFITS AND ENTITLEMENTS	Unemployment compensation; Workers' compensation; Aid to aged, blind and disabled; Social Security
WAGES	Bankruptcy: Earned but unpaid wages owed for 30 days, then greater of 75% or 30 times the minimum hourly wage per week.
MISCELLANEOUS	Business partnership property
WILD CARD	See personal property

In Bankruptcy you must claim the state not the federal expemptions.
(Mississippi Code Sec. 85-3-1; Sec. 85-3-4; Sec. 85-3-17; Sec. 85-3-21.)

MISSOURI

REAL ESTATE	Real property to $8,000, mobile home to $1,000
PERSONAL PROPERTY/ HOUSEHOLD GOODS	Appliances, household goods, clothing, books, crops, animals & musical instruments to $1,000; Jewelry to $500; Motor vehicle to $1,000; Wrongful death recoveries for person you depended on; Burial plot.
INSURANCE AND ANNUITIES	Insurance premium proceeds; Death, disability or illness benefits; Life insurance dividends, loan value or interest; Life insurance.
PENSIONS AND RETIREMENT PLANS	Employees of cities w/100,000+ people; ERISA; Public officers & employees, police, highway & transportation, firefighters; State employees; Teachers
PUBLIC BENEFITS AND ENTITLEMENTS	Veterans' benefits; Workers' compensation; AFDC; Social Security; Unemployment compensation
WAGES	Bankruptcy: Minimum 75% of earned but unpaid wages (90% for head of family); Wages of servant or common laborer to $90
MISCELLANEOUS	Alimony, child support to $500 per month; Business partnership property; Books & tools of trade to $2,000
WILD CARD	$850 of any property if head of family; else $400. Head of family may claim additional $250 per child

In Bankruptcy you must claim the state not the federal exemptions.
(Annotated Missouri Statutes Sec. 513.430; Sec. 513.440; Sec. 513.475; Sec. 525.030.)

MONTANA

REAL ESTATE	Real estate, mobile home to $40,000
PERSONAL PROPERTY/ HOUSEHOLD GOODS	Appliances, household furnishings, goods, animals, crops, musical instruments, books, firearms, clothing & jewelry to $600 each, $4,500 total; Cooperative association shares to $500 value; Motor vehicle to $1,200; Proceeds for damaged or lost exempt property for 6 months after received; Burial place; Food and provisions for 3 months
INSURANCE AND ANNUITIES	Annuity to $350 per month; Disability or illness benefits; medical, surgical or hospital benefits; Group life insurance; Life insurance proceeds if cannot be used to pay beneficiary's creditors; Life insurance proceeds if annual premiums do not exceed $500; Unmatured life insurance contracts to $4,000; Fraternal society benefits
PENSIONS AND RETIREMENT PLANS	ERISA benefits deposited over 1 year before creditor attachment or bankruptcy (in excess of 15% of yearly income); Public employees
PUBLIC BENEFITS AND ENTITLEMENTS	Workers' compensation; Veterans' benefits; Aid to aged, disabled, AFDC; Crime victims' compensation; Social Security; Unemployment compensation; Vocational rehabilitation to the blind
WAGES	Bankruptcy: Minimum 75% of earned but unpaid wages; Judgment creditor: Greater of 75% of your weekly net earnings or $114 per week
MISCELLANEOUS	Alimony, child support; Business partnership property; Books & tools of trade to $3,000

In Bankruptcy you must claim the state not the federal exemptions.
(Montana Code Annotated Sec. 25-13-608;: Sec. 25-13-613; Sec. 25-13-614; Sec. 70-32-104.)

NEBRASKA

REAL ESTATE	$10,000; (no more than 2 lots in city, 160 acres elsewhere). Sale proceeds exempt for 6 months
PERSONAL PROPERTY/ HOUSEHOLD GOODS	Burial place; Clothing; Furniture & kitchen utensils to $1,500; Perpetual care funds; Recovery for personal injury
INSURANCE AND ANNUITIES	Disability benefits to $200 per month; Fraternal benefit society benefits
PENSIONS AND RETIREMENT PLANS	County employees, state and school employees; ERISA; Military disability benefits to $2,000
PUBLIC BENEFITS AND ENTITLEMENTS	Unemployment compensation; Workers' compensation; Aid to disabled, blind, aged, AFDC
WAGES	Bankruptcy: Minimum 85% of earned but unpaid wages or pension payments for head of family; 75% for all others;
MISCELLANEOUS	Business partnership property; Equipment or tools to $1,500
WILD CARD	$2,500 of any personal property if homestead is not claimed; cannot claim wages

In Bankruptcy you must claim the state not the federal exemptions.
(Revised Statutes of Nebraska Sec. 12-517; Sec. 25-1552; Sec. 25-1556; Sec. 25-1558; Sec. 40-101.)

NEVADA

REAL ESTATE	Real property or trailer to $95,000
PERSONAL PROPERTY/ HOUSEHOLD GOODS	Appliances, household goods, furniture, home & yard equipment to $3,000 total; Books to $1,500; Burial place; Funeral service contract; Motor vehicle to $1,500; Heirlooms
INSURANCE AND ANNUITIES	Group life or health policy or proceeds; Benefits from fraternal society ; Annuity to $350 per month; Health proceeds; Life insurance proceeds if you're not the insured; Life insurance policy or proceeds if annual premiums not over $1,000
PENSIONS AND RETIREMENT PLANS	Public employees
PUBLIC BENEFITS AND ENTITLEMENTS	Vocational rehabilitation benefits; Unemployment compensation; Aid to blind, aged, disabled, AFDC
WAGES	Bankruptcy: Minimum 75% of earned but unpaid wages.
MISCELLANEOUS	Business partnership property; Dwelling of miner or prospector; Cars, equipment for mining & mining claim you work to $4,500 total; Farm trucks, stock, equipment & seed to $4,500; Library, equipment, supplies, tools & materials to $4,500; Uniforms, arms & equipment

In Bankruptcy you must claim the state not the federal exemptions.
(Nevada Revised Statutes Sec. 21.090; Sec. 115.010.)

NEW HAMPSHIRE

REAL ESTATE	Real property or portable housing (must own the land it's on) to $30,000

PERSONAL PROPERTY/ HOUSEHOLD GOODS	Beds, bedsteads, bedding, furniture; Sewing maching, cooking utensils needed, cooking & heating stoves, refrigerator; Automobile to $1,000; Bibles & books to $800; Burial place; Jewelry to $500; Proceeds for lost or destroyed exempt property; Clothing; Cow, 6 sheep or fleece; 4 tons of hay; Food & fuel to $400
INSURANCE AND ANNUITIES	Homeowners' insurance proceeds to $1,500 except if homestead property; Fraternal benefits;Firefighter's aid insurance; Life insurance if you're not the insured; Life insurance or endowment proceeds if beneficiary is a married woman
PENSIONS AND RETIREMENT PLANS	Police officers; Firefighters; Public employees; Federal pension
PUBLIC BENEFITS AND ENTITLEMENTS	Workers' compensation; Unemployment compensation; Aid to blind, aged, disabled, AFDC
WAGES	50 times the minimum hourly wage per week.
MISCELLANEOUS	Child support; Business partnership property; Minor child's wages; Tools of the trade to $1,200; Military member's uniforms, arms & equipment

In Bankruptcy you must claim the state not the federal exemptions.
(New Hampshire Revised Statutes Annotated Sec. 480:1; Sec. 511:2; Sec. 512:21.)

NEW JERSEY

PERSONAL PROPERTY/ HOUSEHOLD GOODS	Personal property & corporation shares to $1,000 total; Burial place; Clothing; Furniture & household goods to $1,000
INSURANCE AND ANNUITIES	Annuity contract proceeds to $500 per month; Military disability or death benefits; Disability, death, medical or hospital benefits for civil defense workers; Life insurance proceeds if proceeds cannot be used to pay beneficiary's creditors; Life insurance proceeds if another insured; Fraternal society benefits; Health or disability benefits
PENSIONS AND RETIREMENT PLANS	Alcohol beverage control officers; City boards of health employees; County employees; ERISA; Public employees
PUBLIC BENEFITS AND ENTITLEMENTS	Workers' compensation; Unemployment compensation; Crime victims' compensation; Old-age, permanent disability assistance
WAGES	90% of earned but unpaid wages if income under $7,500; if income over $7,500, court decides amount; Wages or allowances of military personnel
MISCELLANEOUS	Business partnership property

In Bankruptcy you may claim either the state or the federal exemptions.
(New Jersey Statutes Annotated Sec. 2A:17-19; Sec. 2A:17-56; Sec. 2A:26-4.)

NEW MEXICO

REAL ESTATE	Up to $30,000; if jointly owned, up to $30,000 for each owner
PERSONAL PROPERTY/ HOUSEHOLD GOODS	Books, health equipment & furniture; Building supplies; Jewelry to $2,500; Materials, tools & machinery (fuel resource related); Motor vehicle to $4,000; Clothing; Cooperative association shares
INSURANCE AND ANNUITIES	Benevolent association benefits to $5,000; Fraternal society benefits; Life, accident, health or annuity benefits or proceeds

PENSIONS AND RETIREMENT PLANS	Pension or retirement benefits; Public school employees
PUBLIC BENEFITS AND ENTITLEMENTS	Workers' compensation; Unemployment compensation; AFDC; Crime victims' compensation; General assistance; Occupational disease disablement benefits
WAGES	Bankruptcy: Minimum 75% of earned but unpaid wages.
MISCELLANEOUS	Ownership interest in unincorporated association; Business partnership property; $1,500 in tools of the trade
WILD CARD	$500 of any personal property; $2,000 of any property if homestead not claimed

In Bankruptcy you may claim either the state or the federal exemptions.
(New Mexico Statutes Annotated Sec. 42-10-1; Sec. 42-10-2; Sec. 42-10-9; Sec. 42-10-10.)

NEW YORK

REAL ESTATE	Real estate, condo, co-op or mobile home to $10,000
PERSONAL PROPERTY/ HOUSEHOLD GOODS	Schoolbooks; books to $50; pictures; clothing; church pew; stoves; sewing machine; furniture; refrigerator; TV; radio; wedding ring to $5,000 total; Burial place; $2,500 cash or that with annuity totals $5,000 instead of homestead; Recovery for lost earnings needed for support; Personal injury recoveries to $7,500 (not to include pain & suffering); Security deposits; Trust fund principal, 90% of income; Wrongful death recoveries for person you depended on needed for support; Motor vehicle to $2,400; Food for 60 days
INSURANCE AND ANNUITIES	Annuity contract benefits purchased within 6 months of bankruptcy to $5,000; Disability or illness benefits to $400 per month; Fraternal society benefits; Insurance proceeds for damaged exempt property; Life insurance proceeds that cannot pay beneficiary's creditors or if beneficiary is not the insured
PENSIONS AND RETIREMENT PLANS	ERISA, Keoghs and IRAs needed for support
PUBLIC BENEFITS AND ENTITLEMENTS	Workers' compensation; Veterans' benefits; Crime victims' compensation; Aid to blind, aged, disabled, AFDC; Home relief; Social Security; Unemployment compensation
WAGES	90% of earned but unpaid wages received 60 days before creditor attachment or filing for bankruptcy
MISCELLANEOUS	Alimony, child support; Business partnership property; Farm machinery, team, professional furniture, books & instruments to $600 total; Uniforms, arms of military member

In Bankruptcy you must claim the sate not the federal exemptions.
(New York Civil Practice Law and Rules Sec. 5202; Sec. 5206. New York Debtor and Creditor Law Sec. 282-284.)

NORTH CAROLINA

REAL ESTATE	Real or personal property claimed as residence, or burial plot, to $10,000. Tenancy by the entirety property exempt against debt of one spouse. $3,500 of unused homestead may be applied to other property
PERSONAL PROPERTY/ HOUSEHOLD GOODS	Crops, animals,musical instrument, books, clothing, household goods to $3,500 total, plus $750 per dependent (up to $3,000 for dependents); Motor vehicle to $1,500; Wrongful death or injury recoveries for person you depended on; Prescribed health aids
INSURANCE AND ANNUITIES	Benefits from fraternal society; Life insurance
PENSIONS AND RETIREMENT PLANS	Legislators; Municipal, city & county employees
PUBLIC BENEFITS AND ENTITLEMENTS	Unemployment compensation; Workers' compensation; AFDC; Aid to blind; Crime victims' compensation; Special adult assistance
WAGES	Earned but unpaid wages received 60 days before filing for bankruptcy
MISCELLANEOUS	Business partnership property; Books & tools of trade to $750
WILD CARD	$3,500 less any amount claimed for homestead or burial exemption, of any property

n Bankruptcy you must claim the state not the federal exemptions.
(North Carolina Constitution Article X, Sec. 1 & 2. General Statutes of North Carolina Sec. 1c-1601.)

NORTH DAKOTA

REAL ESTATE	Real estate or trailer to $80,000
PERSONAL PROPERTY/ HOUSEHOLD GOODS	Books to $100 & pictures; Clothing; Burial plots, church pew; Cash to $7,500, in lieu of homestead; Crops raised (to 160 acres); Motor vehicle to $1,200; Personal injury recoveries to $7,500 (not pain & suffering); Wrongful death recoveries to $7,500; Head of household not claiming crops may claim $5,000 of any personal property or any of the following: Library & tools of professional to $1,000; Livestock & farm implements to $4,500; Tools & stock in trade to $1,000; Furniture to $1,000; Books & musical instruments to $1,500; Non-head of household not claiming crops may claim $2,500 of any personal property in addition to the above
INSURANCE AND ANNUITIES	Benefits from fraternal society; Life insurance
PENSIONS AND RETIREMENT PLANS	Annuities, pensions, IRAs, Keoghs, & ERISA to $100,000 per plan, total cannot exceed $200,000; Disabled veterans' benefits (not military retirement pay); Public employees
PUBLIC BENEFITS AND ENTITLEMENTS	Unemployment compensation; Workers' compensation; AFDC; Crime victims', Vietnam veterans' adjustment compensation; Social Security
WAGES	Bankruptcy: Minimum 75% of earned but unpaid wages; Judgment creditor: Greater of 75% of your weekly net earnings or $114 per week
MISCELLANEOUS	Business partnership property
WILD CARD	See personal property

In Bankruptcy you must claim the state not the federal exemptions. (North Dakota Century Code Sec. 28-22-02; Sec. 28-22-03.1; Sec. 28-22-04; Sec. 28-22-05; Sec. 32-09.1-.03; Sec. 47-18-01.)

OHIO

REAL ESTATE	Real or personal property claimed as residence to $5,000; tenancy by the entirety property exempt against debt of only one spouse
PERSONAL PROPERTY/ HOUSEHOLD GOODS	Animals, crops, books, musical instruments, clothing, appliances, household goods, furnishings, sporting equipment & firearms to $200 per item to $1,500 total ($2,000 if no homestead claimed);To $400 for 1 item of jewelry; to $200 per item for all other jewelry; Cash, money due within 90 days, bank & security deposits & tax refund to $400 total; Personal injury recoveries to $5,000 (not pain & suffering); Motor vehicle to $1,000; Wrongful death recoveries; Stove & refrigerator to $300 each; Burial place; Prescribed health aids
INSURANCE AND ANNUITIES	Benevolent society benefits; Disability benefits to $600 per month; Benefits from fraternal benefit society; Group life insurance policy or proceeds; Life, endowment or annuity contracts; Life insurance proceeds for a spouse; Life insurance proceeds if proceeds cannot be used to pay beneficiary's creditors; Health and accident benefits
PENSIONS AND RETIREMENT PLANS	ERISA, IRAs, Keoghs; Firefighters', police officers' death benefits and pensions; Public employees; State highway patrol employees; Volunteer firefighters' dependents
PUBLIC BENEFITS AND ENTITLEMENTS	Unemployment compensation; Workers' compensation; AFDC; Crime victim's compensation; Vocational rehabilitation benefits
WAGES	Bankruptcy: Greater of 75% of disposable earnings owed or (if paid weekly) 30 times the federal minimum hourly wage or (if paid biweekly) 60 times the minimum hourly wage, or (if semimonthly) 65 times the minimum hourly wage or (if paid monthly) 130 times the minimum hourly wage; Judgment creditor: Greater of 75% of your weekly net earnings or $114 per week
MISCELLANEOUS	Alimony, child support needed for support; Property of business partnership; Tools of trade to $750
WILD CARD	$400 of any property

In Bankruptcy you must claim the state not the federal exemptions.
(Ohio Revised Code Sec. 2329.66.)

OKLAHOMA

REAL ESTATE	Real property to unlimited value; property cannot exceed 1/4 acre. If property in excess of 1/4 acre, may claim $5,000 on 1 acre in city, town or village, or 160 acres rural
PERSONAL PROPERTY/ HOUSEHOLD GOODS	Books, portraits, pictures; Burial plots; Clothing to $4,000; Furniture; Motor vehicle to $3,000; Personal injury, wrongful death & workers' compensation recoveries to $50,000 total
INSURANCE AND ANNUITIES	Funeral benefits; Life insurance policy or proceeds if another insured; Limited stock insurance benefits; Fraternal society benefits
PENSIONS AND RETIREMENT PLANS	County employees; Disabled veterans; ERISA; Law enforcement employees, police and firefighters; Public employees and teachers; Tax exempt benefits
PUBLIC BENEFITS AND ENTITLEMENTS	Unemployment compensation; Workers' compensation; AFDC; Crime victims' compensation; Social security
WAGES	75% of wages earned 90 days before creditor attachment or filing for bankruptcy

MISCELLANEOUS	Alimony, child support; Business partnership property; Farm tools to $5,000 total

In Bankruptcy you must claim the state not the federal exemptions.
(Oklahoma Statutes Annotated Title 31 Sec. 1 & 2.)

OREGON

REAL ESTATE	Residence to $25,000 ($33,000 for joint owners); Mobile home and property to $23,000 ($30,000 for joint owners); Mobile home without property to $20,000 ($27,000 for joint owners) Sale proceeds to $33,000 exempt 1 year from sale, if you purchase another home
PERSONAL PROPERTY/ HOUSEHOLD GOODS	Bank deposits to $7,500; Books, pictures & musical instruments to $600 total; Burial place; Clothing, jewelry & other personal items to $1,800 total; Domestic animals, poultry to $1,000 with food to last 60 days; Furniture, household items, utensils, radios & TV to $3,000 total; Payments for lost earnings; Personal injury recoveries to $7,500, not to include pain & suffering; Motor vehicle to $1,700; Household provisions and fuel for 60 days; Prescribed health aids
INSURANCE AND ANNUITIES	Annuity contract benefits to $250 per month; Fraternal society benefits; Health or disability proceeds; Life insurance
PENSIONS AND RETIREMENT PLANS	ERISA benefits, if deposited at least 1 year before creditor attachment or filing for bankruptcy, including IRAs, (but not Keoghs); Government employees
PUBLIC BENEFITS AND ENTITLEMENTS	Unemployment compensation; Workers' compensation; AFDC; Aid to disabled, blind, old age; Crime victims' compensation; General assistance; Medical assistance; Vocational rehabilitation
WAGES	Bankruptcy: Minimum of 75% of earned but unpaid wages; Judgment creditor: Greater of 75% of your weekly net earnings or $114 per week; Wages withheld in an employee's bond savings account
MISCELLANEOUS	Alimony, child support; Liquor licenses; Business partnership property; Tools, library to $3,000
WILD CARD	$400 of any property

In Bankruptcy you must claim the state not the federal exemptions.
(Oregon Revised Statutes Sec. 23.160; Sec. 23.164; Sec. 23.185; Sec. 23.200; Sec. 23.240.)

PENNSYLVANIA

REAL ESTATE	None. Tenancy by the entirety property exempt against debt of one spouse
PERSONAL PROPERTY/ HOUSEHOLD GOODS	School books & sewing machines; Clothing
INSURANCE AND ANNUITIES	Group life policy or proceeds; Life insurance annuity contract payments, cash value or proceeds to $100 per month; Life insurance annuity policy, cash value or proceeds; Life insurance proceeds if proceeds cannot be used to pay beneficiary's creditors; Fraternal society benefits; No fault automobile insurance proceeds; Accident or disability benefits
PENSIONS AND RETIREMENT PLANS	County, municipal, and state employees; Private retirement benefits (if proceeds cannot be used to pay beneficiary's creditors); Self-employment benefits
PUBLIC BENEFITS AND ENTITLEMENTS	Unemployment compensation; Workers' compensation; Crime victims' compensation; Veterans' benefits

WAGES	Earned but unpaid wages
MISCELLANEOUS	Business partnership property
WILD CARD	$300 of any property

In Bankruptcy you may claim either the state or the federal exemptions.
(Pennsylvania Consolidated Statutes Annotated Title 42 Sec. 8123, 8124 & 8127.)

RHODE ISLAND

PERSONAL PROPERTY/ HOUSEHOLD GOODS	Furniture to $1,000 total; Books to $300; Burial place; Clothing; Debts due; Certain animals
INSURANCE AND ANNUITIES	Accident or sickness proceeds or benefits; Fraternal society benefits; Life insurance proceeds if beneficiary is not the insured; Temporary disability insurance
PENSIONS AND RETIREMENT PLANS	Private employees; State & municipal employees
PUBLIC BENEFITS AND ENTITLEMENTS	Unemployment compensation; Workers' compensation; Aid to blind, aged, disabled, AFDC; General assistance; State disability benefits; Veterans' disability or survivors' death benefits;
WAGES	Wages to $50; Wages due military member or survivor on active duty; Wages of spouse
MISCELLANEOUS	A minor child's earnings; Business partnership property; Library; Tools of trade to $500

In Bankruptcy you may claim either the state or the federal exemptions.
(General Laws of Rhode Island Sec. 9-26-4.)

SOUTH CAROLINA

REAL ESTATE	Real property to $5,000
PERSONAL PROPERTY/ HOUSEHOLD GOODS	Animals, crops, books, clothing, furnishings, musical instruments to $2,500 total; Burial place to $5,000, if homestead is not claimed; Cash to $1,000, in lieu of burial or homestead exemption; Jewelry to $500; Motor vehicle to $1,200; Personal injury and wrongful death recoveries
INSURANCE AND	Life insurance from person you depended on to $4,000; Life insurance proceeds if proceeds cannot be used to pay beneficiary's creditors; Fraternal society benefits; Disability or illness benefits
PENSIONS AND RETIREMENT PLANS	ERISA; Firefighters and police officers; Public employees
PUBLIC BENEFITS AND ENTITLEMENTS	Unemployment compensation; Workers' compensation; AFDC; Crime victims' compensation; Aid to aged, blind, disabled; Social Security; Veterans' benefits
MISCELLANEOUS	Alimony, child support; Business partnership property; Implements & tools of trade to $750

In Bankruptcy you must claim the state not the federal exemptions.
(Code of Laws of South Carolina Sec. 15-41-200.)

SOUTH DAKOTA

REAL ESTATE	Real property under 1 acre in town or 160 acres elsewhere. Sale proceeds to $30,000 (unlimited if over age 70 or an unmarried widow or widower) exempt for 1 year after sale

PERSONAL PROPERTY/ HOUSEHOLD GOODS	Books, musical instruments to $200, pictures, burial plots, church pew, food, fuel & clothing; Head of family may claim $4,000 of any personal property;Animals and farming machinery to $1,250 total; Furniture and bedding to $200; Professional library & tools to $300; Tools of mechanic & stock in trade; Non-head of family may claim $2,000 of any personal property
INSURANCE AND ANNUITIES	Endowment, life insurance policy, proceeds or cash value to $20,000; Health benefits to $20,000; Fraternal society benefits; Life insurance proceeds if proceeds cannot pay beneficiary's creditors; Life insurance proceeds to $10,000 if beneficiary is surviving spouse or child; Annuity to $250 per month
PENSIONS AND RETIREMENT PLANS	Public employees
PUBLIC BENEFITS AND ENTITLEMENTS	Unemployment compensation; Workers' compensation; AFDC
WAGES	Greater of 80% or 40 times the minimum hourly wage per week, plus $25 a week for each dependent.
MISCELLANEOUS	Business partnership property
WILD CARD	See personal property

In Bankruptcy you must claim the state not the federal exemptions.
(South Dakota Codified Laws Sec. 15-20-12; Sec. 43-31-4; Sec. 43-45-2; Sec. 43-45-4; Sec. 43-45-5.)

TENNESSEE

REAL ESTATE	$5,000; $7,500 for joint owners. Tenancy by the entirety property exempt against debt of one spouse
PERSONAL PROPERTY/ HOUSEHOLD GOODS	School books, portraits; Burial place; Clothing; Payments for lost earnings; Personal injury recoveries to $7,500 (not pain & suffering); Wrongful death recoveries to $10,000
INSURANCE AND ANNUITIES	Fraternal society benefits; Homeowners' insurance proceeds to $5,000; Life insurance; Accident, health or disability benefits
PENSIONS AND RETIREMENT PLANS	ERISA; Public employees; State & local government employees; Teachers
PUBLIC BENEFITS AND ENTITLEMENTS	Unemployment compensation; Workers' compensation; AFDC; Aid to blind, disabled, old age; Crime victims' compensation to $5,000; General assistance; Social Security; Veterans' benefits
WAGES	Bankruptcy: Minimum 75% of earned but unpaid wages; Judgment creditor: Greater of 75% of your weekly net earnings or $114 per week (plus $2.50 per week per child)
MISCELLANEOUS	Alimony owed for 30 days prior; Business partnership property; Tools of trade to $750
WILD CARD	$4,000 of any personal property

In Bankruptcy you must claim the state not the federal exemptions.
(Tennessee Code Annotated Sec. 26-2-102; Sec. 26-2-103; Sec. 26-2-106; Sec. 26-2-111; Sec. 26-2-301; Sec. 26-2-305.)

TEXAS

REAL ESTATE	Property of head of family to $60,000; Property of single adult to $30,000; to 1 acre in town, village, city or 100 acres (200 for families) elsewhere

PERSONAL PROPERTY/ HOUSEHOLD GOODS	Sporting equipment; Clothing; Home furnishings, including heirlooms; Jewelry to $15,000 for family debtor or $7,500 for non-family debtor; Food, livestock and forage; Motor vehicle (2 or 4-wheeled) per debtor who has either a driver's license or a driver; Prescribed health aids; 2 firearms; total includes tools of trade, wages and life insurance cash value.
INSURANCE AND ANNUITIES	Life, health, accident or annuity benefits & cash value; Retired public school employees group insurance; State employee uniform group insurance; State college or university employee benefits; Benefits from fraternal society
PENSIONS AND RETIREMENT PLANS	County & district employees; ERISA government or church benefits, Keoghs and IRAs; Firefighters, police, judges, and teachers; Law enforcement officers' survivors; Municipal employees; State employees
PUBLIC BENEFITS AND ENTITLEMENTS	Unemployment compensation; Workers' compensation; Aid for dependent children; Crime victims' compensation; Medical assistance
WAGES	Earned but unpaid wages
MISCELLANEOUS	Business partnership property; Implements of farming or ranching needed to work; Tools, books and equipment, including boats and vehicles, needed to work

In Bankruptcy you may claim either the state or the federal exemptions.
(Texas Property Code Annotated Sec. 41.001; Sec. 42.001; Sec. 42.002.)

UTAH

REAL ESTATE	Real property or trailer to $8,000; plus $2,000 for spouse & $500 per dependent
PERSONAL PROPERTY/ HOUSEHOLD GOODS	Animals, books & musical instruments to $500 total; Burial place; Bed, bedding, carpets, washer & dryer; Clothing (not furs); Furnishings & appliances to $500; Heirloom to $500; Proceeds for damaged exempt property; Refrigerator, freezer, stove & sewing machine; Personal injury recovery; Wrongful death recoveries
INSURANCE AND ANNUITIES	Fraternal society benefits; Life insurance policy cash surrender value to $1,500; Life insurance proceeds if beneficiary is insured's spouse or dependent; Disability, illness, medical or hospital benefits;
PENSIONS AND RETIREMENT PLANS	ERISA; Public employees; Any pensions needed for support
PUBLIC BENEFITS AND ENTITLEMENTS	Unemployment compensation; Workers' compensation; AFDC; Crime victims' compensation; General assistance; Occupational disease disability benefits; Veterans' benefits
WAGES	Bankruptcy: Minimum 75% of earned but unpaid wages; Judgment creditor: Greater of 75% of your weekly net earnings or $114 per week
MISCELLANEOUS	Alimony needed for support; Child support; Property of business partnership; Books & tools of trade to $1,500; Military property; Motor vehicle to $1,500

In Bankruptcy you must claim the state not the federal exemptions.
(Utah Code Sec. 78-23-3; Sec. 78-23-5; Sec. 78-23-8.)

VERMONT

REAL ESTATE	Real property or mobile home to $30,000; Tenancy by the entirety property exempt against debt of only one spouse

PERSONAL PROPERTY/ HOUSEHOLD GOODS	Furnishings, clothing, books, crops, animals, musical instruments to $2,500 total; Jewelry to $500; wedding ring unlimited; Motor vehicles to $2,500; bank deposits to $700; Stove, refrigerator, water heater & sewing machines; Wrongful death recoveries for person you depended on; Sidearms; Personal injury recoveries
INSURANCE AND ANNUITIES	Group life or health benefits; Fraternal society benefits; Life insurance proceeds if beneficiary is not the insured; Life insurance proceeds if proceeds cannot be used to pay beneficiary's creditors; Annuity benefits to $350 per month
PENSIONS AND RETIREMENT PLANS	Municipal employees; IRAs, Keoghs to $10,000; State employees & teachers; Any pensions
PUBLIC BENEFITS AND ENTITLEMENTS	Unemployment compensation; Workers' compensation; Aid to blind, aged, disabled, AFDC; Crime victims' compensation; General assistance; Social Security; Veterans' benefits
WAGES	Bankruptcy: Minimum 75% of earned but unpaid wages; Judgment creditor: Greater of 75% of your weekly net earnings or $114 per week
MISCELLANEOUS	Alimony, child support needed for support; Business partnership property; Books & tools of trade to $5,000
WILD CARD	$7,000 less any amount of appliances, growing crops, jewelry, motor vehicle & tools of trade claimed, of any property; $400 of any property

In Bankruptcy, you may claim either the state or the federal exemptions.
(Vermont Statutes Annotated Title 12 Sec. 2740; Title 27 Sec. 101.)

VIRGINIA

REAL ESTATE	$5,000; $500 per dependent; Tenancy by the entirety property exempt against debt of one spouse
PERSONAL PROPERTY/ HOUSEHOLD GOODS	Furniture, furnishings & utensils to $5,000; Burial place; Wedding, engagement rings
INSURANCE AND ANNUITIES	Cooperative life insurance benefits; Benefits from fraternal society; Group life insurance policy or proceeds; Industrial sick benefits; Life insurance cash values to $10,000; Life insurance proceeds if beneficiary is not the insured; Burial benefits; Accident or disability benefits
PENSIONS AND RETIREMENT PLANS	County & state employees
PUBLIC BENEFITS AND ENTITLEMENTS	Unemployment compensation;Workers' compensation; Aid to blind, aged, disabled, AFDC; Crime victims' compensation; General assistance
WAGES	Bankruptcy: Minimum 75% of earned but unpaid wages, pension payments.
MISCELLANEOUS	Business partnership property; Boat to $1,000; Tools of mechanic or farmer to $10,000; Uniforms, equipment of military
WILD CARD	$5,000 of personal property, if homestead is not claimed; $2,000, any property of disabled veterans

In Bankruptcy you must claim the state not the federal exemptions.
(Code of Virginia Sec. 34-4; Sec. 34-4.1; Sec. 34-6; Sec. 34-26; Sec. 34-27; Sec. 34-29.)

WASHINGTON

REAL ESTATE	Real property to $30,000
PERSONAL PROPERTY/ HOUSEHOLD GOODS	Furniture, household goods to $2,700 total; Clothing, only $1000 in furs & jewelry; Food & fuel; Books to $1,500; Burial place; 2 motor vehicles to $2,500 (combined).

INSURANCE AND ANNUITIES	Fire insurance proceeds for destroyed exemption; Benefits from fraternal benefit society;Life insurance proceeds if beneficiary is not the insured; Disability proceeds or benefits; Annuity to $250 per month
PENSIONS AND RETIREMENT PLANS	Public employees; ERISA,IRAs; State patrol officers; Volunteer firefighters
PUBLIC BENEFITS AND ENTITLEMENTS	Unemployment compensation; Workers' compensation; Child welfare; (AFDC); Crime victims' compensation; General assistance; Old-age assistance
WAGES	Bankruptcy: Minimum 75% of earned but unpaid wages.
MISCELLANEOUS	Business partnership property; Farm trucks, stock, equipment of farmer to $5,000; Library, office furniture, equipment & supplies of professional to $5,000; Tools & materials used in trade to $5,000
WILD CARD	$1000 of any personal property (no more than $100 in cash, bank deposits, bonds, stocks & securities)

In Bankruptcy you may claim either the state or the federal exemptions.
(Revised Code of Washington Annotated Sec. 6.12.050; Sec. 6.16.020; Sec. 7.33.280.)

WEST VIRGINIA

REAL ESTATE	Real or personal property claimed as residence to $5,000; unused homestead may be applied to other property
PERSONAL PROPERTY/ HOUSEHOLD GOODS	Unripe crops, Clothing, appliances, books, furnishings, musical instruments to $200 per item, $1,000 total; Burial plot to $7,500, if homestead not claimed; Payment for lost earnings; Motor vehicle to $1,200; Jewelry to $500; Personal injury recoveries to $7,500 (not pain & suffering); Wrongful death recoveries needed for support
INSURANCE AND ANNUITIES	Benefits from fraternal society; Group life insurance policy or proceeds; Health or disability benefits; Life insurance to $4,000, from person you depended on; Life insurance proceeds unless you are both policy owner and beneficiary; Life insurance proceeds or cash value if beneficiary is married woman
PENSIONS AND RETIREMENT PLANS	ERISA; Public employees
PUBLIC BENEFITS AND ENTITLEMENTS	Unemployment compensation; Workers' compensation; Aid to blind, aged, disabled, AFDC; Crime victims' compensation; General assistance; Social Security; Veterans' benefits;
WAGES	Bankruptcy: 80% of earned but unpaid wages.
MISCELLANEOUS	Alimony, child support; Business partnership property; Tools of trade to $750
WILD CARD	$400 of any property; Unused portion of homestead or burial exemption

In Bankruptcy you must claim the state not the federal exemptions.
(West Virginia Code Sec. 38-10-4.)

WISCONSIN

REAL ESTATE	$40,000; Proceeds exempt for 2 years
PERSONAL PROPERTY/ HOUSEHOLD GOODS	Motor vehicle to $1,200 plus any unused consumer goods exemption; Food & fuel; Bank deposits to $1,000; Beds, clothing, books, pictures, radio,TV, burial place, church pew, patents, cooking utensils & furniture to $5,000; Alimony and child support; Wrongful death or personal injury recoveries needed for support

INSURANCE AND ANNUITIES	Federal disability insurance; Fire proceeds of destroyed exempt property; Health, accident or disability benefits to $150/month; Life insurance policy or proceeds to $4,000; Life insurance proceeds; Benefits from fraternal society
PENSIONS AND RETIREMENT PLANS	Public employees; Firefighters, police pension funds: Military pensions; Retirement benefits
PUBLIC BENEFITS AND ENTITLEMENTS	Workers' compensation; Veterans' benefits; AFDC, other social services payments; Unemployment compensation; Crime victim awards
WAGES	Wages for 30 days; if you have dependents, $120 plus $20 per dependent, not to exceed 75% of your wages. No dependents, no less than $75 nor more than $100
MISCELLANEOUS	Business partnership property; Farm utensils, small tools & implements to $300, tractor to $1,500; Business and farm property and professional books to $7,500; Printing materials of printer or publisher to $1,500; $400 for wages due workers; Tools, implements, stock in trade of mechanic, miner, merchant or trader to $200; Uniform, equipment of national guardsman

In Bankruptcy, you may claim either the state or the federal exemptions.
(Wisconsin Statutes Annotated Sec. 815.18; Sec. 815.20.)

WYOMING

REAL ESTATE	Real property to $10,000 (mobile trailer to $6,000). Tenancy by the entirety property exempt against debt of one spouse
PERSONAL PROPERTY/ HOUSEHOLD GOODS	Furniture, household articles & food to $2,000 per person in the home; Books; Burial place; Funeral contract; Clothing & wedding rings up to $1,000
INSURANCE AND ANNUITIES	Benefits from fraternal society; Group life or disability policy or proceeds; Life insurance proceeds (if beneficiary is not the insured); Life insurance proceeds not used to pay beneficiary's creditors; Disability benefits; Annuity to $350 per month
PENSIONS AND RETIREMENT PLANS	Firefighters; Police officers; Public employees
PUBLIC BENEFITS AND ENTITLEMENTS	Unemployment compensation; Workers' compensation; AFDC; Crime victims' compensation; General assistance
WAGES	Bankruptcy: Minimum 75% of earned but unpaid wages; Judgment creditor: Greater of 75% of your weekly net earnings or $114 per week; Wages of work release prisoners; Earnings of national guard members
MISCELLANEOUS	Liquor licenses; Business partnership property; Library & equipment of professional to $2,000 or, tools, motor vehicle, implements, team & stock in trade to $2,000

In Bankruptcy you must claim the state not the federal exemptions.
(Wyoming Statutes Annotated Sec. 1-17-411; Sec. 1-20-101; Sec. 1-20-105; Sec. 1-20-106.)

How To Save On Attorney Fees

Millions of Americans know they need legal protection, whether it's to get agreements in writing, protect themselves from lawsuits, or document business transactions. But too often these basic but important legal matters are neglected because of something else millions of Americans know: legal services are expensive.

They don't have to be. In response to the demand for affordable legal protection and services, there are now specialized clinics that process simple documents. Paralegals help people prepare legal claims on a freelance basis. People find they can handle their own legal affairs with do-it-yourself legal guides and kits. Indeed, this book is a part of this growing trend.

Highlight

When are these alternatives to a lawyer appropriate? If you hire an attorney, how can you make sure you're getting good advice for a reasonable fee? Most importantly, do you know how to lower your legal expenses?

When are these alternatives to a lawyer appropriate? If you hire an attorney, how can you make sure you're getting good advice for a reasonable fee? Most importantly, do you know how to lower your legal expenses?

When there is no alternative

Make no mistake: serious legal matters require a lawyer. The tips in this book can help you reduce your legal fees, but there is no alternative to good professional legal services in certain circumstances:

- When you are charged with a felony, you are a repeat offender, or jail is possible.
- When a substantial amount of money or property is at stake in a lawsuit.
- When you are a party in an adversarial divorce or custody case.
- When you are an alien facing deportation.

- When you are the plaintiff in a personal injury suit that involves large sums of money.
- When you're involved in very important transactions.

Are you sure you want to take it to court?

Consider the following questions before you pursue legal action:

Highlight

Even with a strong case, you may save money by not going to court.

What are your financial resources?

Money buys experienced attorneys, and experience wins over first-year lawyers and public defenders. Even with a strong case, you may save money by not going to court. Yes, people win millions in court. But for every big winner there are ten plaintiffs who either lose or win so little that litigation wasn't worth their effort.

Do you have the time and energy for a trial?

Courts are overbooked, and by the time your case is heard your initial zeal may have grown cold. If you can, make a reasonable settlement out of court. On personal matters, like a divorce or custody case, consider the emotional toll on all parties. Any legal case will affect you in some way. You will need time away from work. A newsworthy case may bring press coverage. Your loved ones, too, may face publicity. There is usually good reason to settle most cases quickly, quietly, and economically.

How can you settle your disputes without litigation?

Consider *mediation.* In mediation, each party pays half the mediator's fee and, together, they attempt to work out a compromise informally. *Binding arbitration* is another alternative. For a small fee, a trained specialist serves as judge, hears both sides, and hands down a ruling that both parties have agreed to accept.

So you need an attorney

Having done your best to avoid litigation, if you still find yourself headed for court, you will need an attorney. To get the right attorney at a reasonable cost, be guided by these four questions:

What type of case is it?

You don't seek a foot doctor for a toothache. Find an attorney experienced in your type of legal problem. If you can get recommendations from clients who have recently won similar cases, do so.

Where will the trial be held?

You want a lawyer familiar with that court system and one who knows the court personnel and the local protocol—which can vary from one locality to another.

Should you hire a large or small firm?

Hiring a senior partner at a large and prestigious law firm sounds reassuring, but chances are the actual work will be handled by associates—at high rates. Small firms may give your case more attention but, with fewer resources, take longer to get the work done.

Highlight

High fees may reflect a firm's luxurious offices, high-paid staff and unmonitored expenses, while low estimates may mean "unexpected" costs later.

What can you afford?

Hire an attorney you can afford, of course, but know what a fee quote includes. High fees may reflect a firm's luxurious offices, high-paid staff and unmonitored expenses, while low estimates may mean "unexpected" costs later. Ask for a written estimate of all costs and anticipated expenses.

How to find a good lawyer

Whether you need an attorney quickly or you're simply open to future possibilities, here are seven nontraditional methods for finding your lawyer:

1. ***Word of mouth:*** Successful lawyers develop reputations. Your friends, business associates and other professionals are potential referral sources. But beware of hiring a friend. Keep the client-attorney relationship strictly business.
2. ***Directories:*** The Yellow Pages and the Martin-Hubbell Lawyer Directory (in your local library) can help you locate a lawyer with the right education, background and expertise for your case.
3. ***Databases:*** A paralegal should be able to run a quick computer search of local attorneys for you using the Westlaw or Lexis database.
4. ***State bar association:*** Bar associations are listed in phone books. Along with lawyer referrals, your bar association can direct you to low-cost legal clinics or specialists in your area.
5. ***Law schools:*** Did you know that a legal clinic run by a law school gives law students hands-on experience? This may fit your legal needs. A third-year law student loaded with enthusiasm and a little experience might fill the bill quite inexpensively—or even for free.
6. ***Advertisements:*** Ads are a lawyer's business card. If a "TV attorney" seems to have a good track record with your kind of case, why not call? Just don't be swayed by the glamour of a high-

profile attorney.

7. ***Your own ad:*** A small ad describing the qualifications and legal expertise you're seeking, placed in a local bar association journal, may get you just the lead you need.

How to hire and work with your attorney

No matter how you hear about an attorney, you must interview him or her in person. Call the office during business hours and ask to speak to the attorney directly. Then explain your case briefly and mention how you obtained the attorney's name. If the attorney sounds interested and knowledgeable, arrange for a visit.

Highlight

Explain your case briefly and mention how you obtained the attorney's name. If the attorney sounds interested and knowledgeable, arrange for a visit.

The ten-point visit:

1. Note the address. This is a good indication of the rates to expect.
2. Note the condition of the offices. File-laden desks and poorly maintained work space may indicate a poorly run firm.
3. Look for up-to-date computer equipment and an adequate complement of support personnel.
4. Note the appearance of the attorney. How will he or she impress a judge or jury?
5. Is the attorney attentive? Does the attorney take notes, ask questions, follow up on points you've mentioned?
6. Ask what schools he or she has graduated from, and feel free to check credentials with the state bar association.
7. Does the attorney have a good track record with your type of case?
8. Does he or she explain legal terms to you in plain English?
9. Are the firm's costs reasonable?
10. Will the attorney provide references?

Hiring the attorney

Having chosen your attorney, make sure all the terms are agreeable. Send letters to any other attorneys you have interviewed, thanking them for their time and interest in your case and explaining that you have retained another attorney's services.

Request a letter from your new attorney outlining your retainer agreement. The letter should list all fees you will be responsible for as well as the billing arrangement. Did you arrange to pay in installments? This should be noted in your retainer agreement.

Controlling legal costs

Highlight

Don't be afraid to question legal bills. It's your case and your money!

Legal fees and expenses can get out of control easily, but the client who is willing to put in the effort can keep legal costs manageable. Work out a budget with your attorney. Create a timeline for your case. Estimate the costs involved in each step.

Legal fees can be straightforward. Some lawyers charge a fixed rate for a specific project. Others charge contingency fees (they collect a percentage of your recovery, usually 35-50 percent, if you win and nothing if you lose). But most attorneys prefer to bill by the hour. Expenses can run the gamut, with one hourly charge for taking depositions and another for making copies.

Have your attorney give you a list of charges for services rendered and an itemized monthly bill. The bill should explain the service performed, who performed the work, when the service was provided, how long it took, and how the service benefits your case.

Ample opportunity abounds in legal billing for dishonesty and greed. There is also plenty of opportunity for knowledgeable clients to cut their bills significantly if they know what to look for. Asking the right questions and setting limits on fees is smart and can save you a bundle. Don't be afraid to question legal bills. It's your case and your money!

When the bill arrives

- ***Retainer fees:*** You should already have a written retainer agreement. Ideally, the retainer fee applies toward case costs, and your agreement puts that in writing. Protect yourself by escrowing the retainer fee until the case has been handled to your satisfaction.
- ***Office visit charges:*** Track your case and all documents, correspondence, and bills. Diary all dates, deadlines and questions you want to ask your attorney during your next office visit. This keeps expensive office visits focused and productive, with more accomplished in less time. If your attorney charges less for phone consultations than office visits, reserve visits for those tasks that must be done in person.

- ***Phone bills:*** This is where itemized bills are essential. Who made the call, who was spoken to, what was discussed, when was the call made, and how long did it last? Question any charges that seem unnecessary or excessive (over 60 minutes).
- ***Administrative costs:*** Your case may involve hundreds, if not thousands, of documents: motions, affidavits, depositions, interrogatories, bills, memoranda, and letters. Are they all necessary? Understand your attorney's case strategy before paying for an endless stream of costly documents.
- ***Associate and paralegal fees:*** Note in your retainer agreement which staff people will have access to your file. Then you'll have an informed and efficient staff working on your case, and you'll recognize their names on your bill. Of course, your attorney should handle the important part of your case, but less costly paralegals or associates may handle routine matters more economically. Note: Some firms expect their associates to meet a quota of billable hours, although the time spent is not always warranted. Review your bill. Does the time spent make sense for the document in question? Are several staff involved in matters that should be handled by one person? Don't be afraid to ask questions. And withhold payment until you have satisfactory answers.

Highlight

Note in your retainer agreement which staff people will have access to your file. Then you'll have an informed and efficient staff working on your case, and you'll recognize their names on your bill.

- ***Court stenographer fees:*** Depositions and court hearings require costly transcripts and stenographers. This means added expenses. Keep an eye on these costs.
- ***Copying charges:*** Your retainer fee should limit the number of copies made of your complete file. This is in your legal interest, because multiple files mean multiple chances others may access your confidential information. It is also in your financial interest, because copying costs can be astronomical.
- ***Fax costs:*** As with the phone and copier, the fax can easily run up costs. Set a limit.
- ***Postage charges:*** Be aware of how much it costs to send a legal document overnight, or a registered letter. Offer to pick up or deliver expensive items when it makes sense.
- ***Filing fees:*** Make it clear to your attorney that you want to minimize the number of court filings in your case. Watch your bill and question any filing that seems unnecessary.
- ***Document production fee:*** Turning over documents to your

Highlight

Surprise costs are so routine they're predictable. Budget a few thousand dollars over what you estimate your case will cost. It usually is needed.

opponent is mandatory and expensive. If you're faced with reproducing boxes of documents, consider having the job done by a commercial firm rather than your attorney's office.

- ***Research and investigations:*** Pay only for photographs that can be used in court. Can you hire a photographer at a lower rate than what your attorney charges? Reserve that right in your retainer agreement. Database research can also be extensive and expensive; if your attorney uses Westlaw or Nexis, set limits on the research you will pay for.
- ***Expert witnesses:*** Question your attorney if you are expected to pay for more than a reasonable number of expert witnesses. Limit the number to what is essential to your case.
- ***Technology costs:*** Avoid videos, tape recordings, and graphics if you can use old-fashioned diagrams to illustrate your case.
- ***Travel expenses:*** Travel expenses for those connected to your case can be quite costly unless you set a maximum budget. Check all travel-related items on your bill, and make sure they are appropriate. Always question why the travel is necessary before you agree to pay for it.
- ***Appeals costs:*** Losing a case often means an appeal, but weigh the costs involved before you make that decision. If money is at stake, do a cost-benefit analysis to see if an appeal is financially justified.
- ***Monetary damages:*** Your attorney should be able to help you estimate the total damages you will have to pay if you lose a civil case. Always consider settling out of court rather than proceeding to trial when the trial costs will be high.
- ***Surprise costs:*** Surprise costs are so routine they're predictable. The judge may impose unexpected court orders on one or both sides, or the opposition will file an unexpected motion that increases your legal costs. Budget a few thousand dollars over what you estimate your case will cost. It usually is needed.
- ***Padded expenses:*** Assume your costs and expenses are legitimate. But some firms do inflate expenses—office supplies, database searches, copying, postage, phone bills—to bolster their bottom line. Request copies of bills your law firm receives from support services. If you are not the only client represented on a bill, determine those charges related to your case.

Keeping it legal without a lawyer

The best way to save legal costs is to avoid legal problems. There are hundreds of ways to decrease your chances of lawsuits and other nasty legal encounters. Most simply involve a little common sense. You can also use your own initiative to find and use the variety of self-help legal aid available to consumers.

11 situations in which you may not need a lawyer

Highlight

The best way to save legal costs is to avoid legal problems.

1. ***No-fault divorce:*** Married couples with no children, minimal property, and no demands for alimony can take advantage of divorce mediation services. A lawyer should review your divorce agreement before you sign it, but you will have saved a fortune in attorney fees. A marital or family counselor may save a seemingly doomed marriage, or help both parties move beyond anger to a calm settlement. Either way, counseling can save you money.
2. ***Wills:*** Do-it-yourself wills and living trusts are ideal for people with estates of less than $600,000. Even if an attorney reviews your final documents, a will kit allows you to read the documents, ponder your bequests, fill out sample forms, and discuss your wishes with your family at your leisure, without a lawyer's meter running.
3. ***Incorporating:*** Incorporating a small business can be done by any business owner. Your state government office provides the forms and instructions necessary. A visit to your state offices will probably be necessary to perform a business name check. A fee of $100-$200 is usually charged for processing your Articles of Incorporation. The rest is paperwork: filling out forms correctly; holding regular, official meetings; and maintaining accurate records.
4. ***Routine business transactions:*** Copyrights, for example, can be applied for by asking the US Copyright Office for the appropriate forms and brochures. The same is true of the US Patent and Trademark Office. If your business does a great deal of document preparation and research, hire a certified paralegal rather than paying an attorney's rates. Consider mediation or binding arbitration rather than going to court for a business dispute. Hire a human resources/benefits administrator to head off disputes

concerning discrimination or other employee charges.

5. ***Repairing bad credit:*** When money matters get out of hand, attorneys and bankruptcy should not be your first solution. Contact a credit counseling organization that will help you work out manageable payment plans so that everyone wins. It can also help you learn to manage your money better. A good company to start with is the Consumer Credit Counseling Service, 1-800-388-2227.

Highlight

If your business does a great deal of document preparation and research, hire a certified paralegal rather than paying an attorney's rates.

6. ***Small Claims Court:*** For legal grievances amounting to a few thousand dollars in damages, represent yourself in Small Claims Court. There is a small filing fee, forms to fill out, and several court visits necessary. If you can collect evidence, state your case in a clear and logical presentation, and come across as neat, respectful and sincere, you can succeed in Small Claims Court.
7. ***Traffic Court:*** Like Small Claims Court, Traffic Court may show more compassion to a defendant appearing without an attorney. If you are ticketed for a minor offense and want to take it to court, you will be asked to plead guilty or not guilty. If you plead guilty, you can ask for leniency in sentencing by presenting mitigating circumstances. Bring any witnesses who can support your story, and remember that presentation (some would call it acting ability) is as important as fact.
8. ***Residential zoning petition:*** If a homeowner wants to open a home business, build an addition, or make other changes that may affect his or her neighborhood, town approval is required. But you don't need a lawyer to fill out a zoning variance application, turn it in, and present your story at a public hearing. Getting local support before the hearing is the best way to assure a positive vote; contact as many neighbors as possible to reassure them that your plans won't adversely affect them or the neighborhood.
9. ***Government benefit applications:*** Applying for veterans' or unemployment benefits may be daunting, but the process doesn't require legal help. Apply for either immediately upon becoming eligible. Note: If your former employer contests your application for unemployment benefits and you have to defend yourself at a hearing, you may want to consider hiring an attorney.
10. ***Receiving government files:*** The Freedom of Information Act gives every American the right to receive copies of government information

about him or her. Write a letter to the appropriate state or federal agency, noting the precise information you want. List each document in a separate paragraph. Mention the Freedom of Information Act, and state that you will pay any expenses. Close with your signature and the address the documents should be sent to. An approved request may take six months to arrive. If it is refused on the grounds that the information is classified or violates another's privacy, send a letter of appeal explaining why the released information would not endanger anyone. Enlist the support of your local state or federal representative, if possible, to smooth the approval process.

11. ***Citizenship:*** Arriving in the United States to work and become a citizen is a process tangled in bureaucratic red tape, but it requires more perseverance than legal assistance. Immigrants can learn how to obtain a "Green Card," under what circumstances they can work, and what the requirements of citizenship are by contacting the Immigration Services or reading a good self-help book.

Highlight

Arriving in the United States to work and become a citizen is a process tangled in bureaucratic red tape, but it requires more perseverance than legal assistance.

Save more; it's E-Z

When it comes to saving attorneys' fees, E-Z Legal Forms is the consumer's best friend. America's largest publisher of self-help legal products offers legally valid forms for virtually every situation. E-Z Legal Kits and E-Z Legal Guides include all necessary forms with a simple-to-follow manual of instructions or a layman's book. E-Z Legal Books are a legal library of forms and documents for everyday business and personal needs. E-Z Legal Software provides those same forms on disk for customized documents at the touch of the keyboard.

You can add to your legal savvy and your ability to protect yourself, your loved ones, your business and your property with a range of self-help legal titles available through E-Z Legal Forms. See the product descriptions and order form at the back of this guide.

(*How To Save On Attorney Fees* was compiled and written by Valerie Hope Goldstein.)

Save on legal fees

with software and books
from E-Z Legal and Garrett Publishing
available at your nearest bookstore, or call 1-800-822-4566

Stock No.: LA101
$24.95 8.5" x 11"
500 pages Soft cover
ISBN 1-56382-101-X

The E•Z Legal Advisor

The book that saves legal fees every time it's opened.

Here, in *The E•Z Legal Advisor*, are fast answers to 90% of the legal questions anyone is ever likely to ask, such as:

- How can I control my neighbor's pet?
- Can I change my name?
- When is a marriage common law?
- When should I incorporate my business?
- Is a child responsible for his bills?
- Who owns a husband's gifts to his wife?
- How do I become a naturalized citizen?
- Should I get my divorce in Nevada?
- Can I write my own will?
- Who is responsible when my son drives my car?
- How does my uncle get a Green Card?
- What are the rights of a non-smoker?
- Do I have to let the police search my car?
- What is sexual harassment?
- When is euthanasia legal?
- What repairs must my landlord make?
- What's the difference between fair criticism and slander?
- When can I get my deposit back?
- Can I sue the federal government?
- Am I responsible for a drunk guest's auto accident?
- Is a hotel liable if it does not honor a reservation?
- Does my car fit the lemon law?

Whether for personal or business use, this 500-page information-packed book helps the layman safeguard his property, avoid disputes, comply with legal obligations, and enforce his rights. Hundreds of cases illustrate thousands of points of law, each clearly and completely explained.

E•Z LEGAL BOOKS®

E•Z LEGAL BOOKS
...when you need it in writing!
301
Legal Forms and Agreements
• Ironclad personal, property and business protection
• Saves legal fees
• Perforated pages for easy record keeping
• Valid in all 50 states

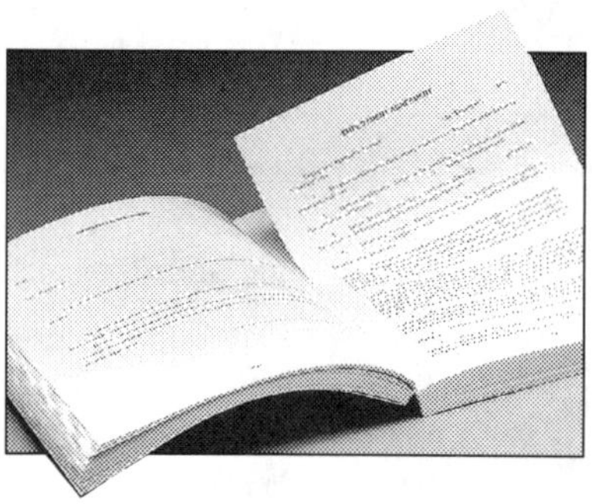

E◆Z Legal® Software

Put a lawyer in your computer!

Put a lawyer in your computer with E•Z Legal Software

Five new programs let you create customized legal documents, business forms, notices and letters instantly. Includes simple user's manual and $3^1/_2$-inch disks ($5^1/_4$-inch disk available at no charge). Two operating systems available: DOS-based and Windows.™ Online help available from anywhere in the program.

FAMILY RECORD ORGANIZER

Maintain household records and document every aspect of your life.

BUSINESS LAWYER

Ironclad legal protection for family, property and business.

CORPORATE SECRETARY

Prepare and maintain up-to-date corporate records.

PERSONNEL DIRECTOR

Forms, letters and documents necessary to manage employees effectively and efficiently.

CREDIT MANAGER

A complete credit and collection system to help you get paid every time.

Available at office supply stores, or call 1-800-822-4566.

Index